BEST-LOVED

QUICK fixes FROM MIXES

Publications International, Ltd.

Favorite Brand Name Recipes at www.fbnr.com

Microwave Cooking: Microwave ovens vary in wattage. Use the cooking times as guidelines and check for doneness before adding more time.

Preparation/Cooking Times: Preparation times are based on the approximate amount of time required to assemble the recipe before cooking, baking, chilling or serving. These times include preparation steps such as measuring, chopping and mixing. The fact that some preparations and cooking can be done simultaneously is taken into account. Preparation of optional ingredients and serving suggestions is not included.

contents

pg. 22

pg. 106

pg. 202

Express Lane Appetizers   4

Hurry-Up Soups & Stews   30

Super Speedy Salads   56

Quick-Fix Casseroles & Skillets   82

No-Fuss Family Favorites   120

Oh-So-Easy Side Dishes   158

Almost Homemade Cakes   186

Deliciously Simple Desserts   216

Acknowledgments   247

Index   248

Roasted Red Pepper Spread *(page 6)*

express lane
appetizers

Bite Size Tacos

Prep Time: 5 minutes   Cook Time: 15 minutes

1 pound ground beef
1 package (1.25 ounces) taco
   seasoning mix
2 cups **French's**® French Fried
   Onions, divided
¾ cup water
¼ cup chopped fresh cilantro
32 bite-size round tortilla chips
¾ cup sour cream
1 cup (4 ounces) shredded Cheddar
   cheese

Makes 8 appetizer servings

1. Cook beef in nonstick skillet over medium-high heat 5 minutes or until browned; drain. Stir in taco seasoning mix, *1 cup* French Fried Onions, water and cilantro. Simmer 5 minutes or until flavors are blended, stirring often.

2. Preheat oven to 350°F. Arrange tortilla chips on foil-lined baking sheet. Top with beef mixture, sour cream, remaining onions and cheese.

3. Bake 5 minutes or until cheese is melted and onions are golden.

Roasted Red Pepper Spread

1 cup roasted red peppers, rinsed
   and drained
1 package (8 ounces) cream cheese,
   softened
1 packet (1 ounce) HIDDEN VALLEY®
   The Original Ranch® Salad
   Dressing & Seasoning Mix
Baguette slices and sliced ripe
   olives (optional)

Makes 2 cups spread

Blot dry red peppers. In a food processor fitted with a metal blade, combine peppers, cream cheese and salad dressing & seasoning mix; process until smooth. Spread on baguette slices and garnish with olives, if desired.

Bite Size Tacos

Savory Chicken Satay

Prep Time: 15 minutes   Cook Time: 8 minutes

1 envelope LIPTON® RECIPE
    SECRETS® Onion Soup Mix
¼ cup BERTOLLI® Olive Oil
2 tablespoons firmly packed brown
    sugar
2 tablespoons SKIPPY® Peanut Butter
1 pound boneless, skinless chicken
    breasts, pounded and cut into
    thin strips
12 to 16 large wooden skewers,
    soaked in water

Makes 12 to 16 appetizers

1. In large plastic bag, combine soup mix, oil, brown sugar and peanut butter. Add chicken and toss to coat well. Seal bag and marinate in refrigerator 30 minutes.

2. Remove chicken from marinade, discarding marinade. On skewers, thread chicken, weaving back and forth.

3. Grill or broil skewers until chicken is thoroughly cooked. Serve with your favorite dipping sauces.

Baked Spinach Feta Dip

Prep Time: 5 Minutes   Cook Time: 35 Minutes

1 cup HELLMANN'S® or BEST
    FOODS® Real Mayonnaise
1 container (16 ounces) sour cream
1 package (10 ounces) frozen
    chopped spinach, thawed
    and squeezed dry
1 package KNORR® Spring
    Vegetable recipe mix
3 green onions, sliced
1 container (4 ounces) feta cheese,
    crumbled

Makes about 4 cups dip

1. Preheat oven to 350°F.

2. In 1½-quart casserole, combine all ingredients. Bake 35 minutes or until heated through. Serve with pita chips or in phyllo cups.

Savory Chicken Satay

Original Ranch® Spinach Dip

1 container (16 ounces) sour cream
 (2 cups)
1 box (10 ounces) frozen chopped
 spinach, thawed and squeezed
 dry
1 can (8 ounces) water chestnuts,
 rinsed, drained and chopped
1 packet (1 ounce) HIDDEN VALLEY®
 The Original Ranch® Salad
 Dressing & Seasoning Mix
1 loaf round French bread
 Fresh vegetables, for dipping

Makes 2½ cups dip

Stir together sour cream, spinach, water chestnuts and salad dressing & seasoning mix. Chill 30 minutes. Just before serving, cut top off bread and remove center, reserving firm bread pieces. Fill bread bowl with dip. Cut reserved bread into cubes. Serve dip with bread and vegetables.

Sausage Pinwheels

 2 cups biscuit mix
½ cup milk
¼ cup butter or margarine, melted
1 pound BOB EVANS® Original
 Recipe Roll Sausage

Makes 48 pinwheels

Combine biscuit mix, milk and butter in large bowl until blended. Refrigerate 30 minutes. Divide dough into two portions. Roll out one portion dough on floured surface to ⅛-inch-thick rectangle, about 10×7 inches. Spread with half the sausage. Roll lengthwise into long roll. Repeat with remaining dough and sausage. Place rolls in freezer until firm enough to cut easily. Preheat oven to 400°F. Cut rolls into thin slices. Place on *ungreased* baking sheets. Bake 15 minutes or until golden brown. Serve hot. Refrigerate leftovers.

Note: This recipe can be doubled. Refreeze after slicing. When ready to serve, thaw slices in refrigerator and bake.

Original Ranch® Spinach Dip

Crispy Tortilla Chicken

1 ½ cups crushed tortilla chips
1 package (about 1 ounce) taco
    seasoning mix
24 chicken drummettes
    (about 2 pounds)
    Salsa (optional)

Makes 2 dozen appetizers

1. Preheat oven to 350°F. Spray large rimmed baking sheet with nonstick cooking spray.

2. Combine tortilla chips and taco seasoning in large shallow bowl. Coat chicken with crumb mixture, turning to coat all sides. Shake off excess crumbs; place chicken on prepared baking sheet.

3. Bake about 40 minutes or until chicken is no longer pink in center. Serve with salsa, if desired.

Variation: The recipe can also be prepared using 1 pound boneless skinless chicken breasts cut into 1-inch strips. Bake at 350°F about 20 minutes or until chicken is no longer pink in center.

Beer Cheese Dip

2 cups (8 ounces) shredded Cheddar
    cheese
2 packages (8 ounces each) cream
    cheese, softened
1 packet (1 ounce) HIDDEN VALLEY®
    The Original Ranch® Salad
    Dressing & Seasoning Mix
½ to ¾ cup beer
    Chopped green onion
    Additional Cheddar cheese

Makes about 3 cups dip

In medium bowl, combine Cheddar cheese, cream cheese and salad dressing & seasoning mix. Gradually stir in beer until mixture is to desired consistency. Garnish with green onion and additional Cheddar cheese. Serve with pretzels or assorted fresh vegetables, if desired.

Crispy Tortilla Chicken

Party Stuffed Pinwheels

1 envelope LIPTON® RECIPE
 SECRETS® Savory Herb
 with Garlic Soup Mix*
1 package (8 ounces) cream cheese,
 softened
1 cup shredded mozzarella cheese
 (about 4 ounces)
2 tablespoons milk
1 tablespoon grated Parmesan
 cheese
2 packages (10 ounces each)
 refrigerated pizza crust

*Also terrific with LIPTON® RECIPE
SECRETS® Onion Soup Mix.*

Makes 32 pinwheels

1. Preheat oven to 425°F. In medium bowl, combine all
ingredients except pizza crusts; set aside.

2. Unroll pizza crusts, then top evenly with filling. Roll up,
starting at longest side, jelly-roll style. Cut each roll into
16 rounds. (If rolled pizza crust is too soft to cut, refrigerate
or freeze until firm.)

3. On baking sheet sprayed with nonstick cooking spray,
arrange rounds cut side down.

4. Bake, uncovered, 13 minutes or until golden brown.

Appetizer Chicken Wings

Prep Time: 15 minutes   Cook Time: 60 minutes

½ cup KARO® Light or Dark Corn
 Syrup
2½ to 3 pounds (12 to 14) chicken
 wings
1 cup (8 ounces) fat-free French
 dressing
1 package (1.4 ounces) French
 onion soup, dip and recipe mix
1 tablespoon Worcestershire sauce

Makes 24 servings

Cut tips from wings and discard. Cut wings apart at joints
and arrange in 13×9×2-inch baking pan lined with foil.

In medium bowl, mix dressing, corn syrup, recipe mix and
Worcestershire sauce; pour over wings.

Bake in 350°F oven 1 hour, stirring once, or until wings
are tender.

Party Stuffed Pinwheels

Mini Taco Quiches

Prep Time: 20 minutes   Cook Time: 30 minutes

1 pound lean ground beef
⅓ cup chopped onions
1 can (8 ounces) tomato sauce
⅓ cup sliced black olives
1 package (1¼ ounces) taco
    seasoning mix
2 tablespoons **Frank's® RedHot®**
    Original Cayenne Pepper Sauce
1 egg, beaten
4 (10-inch) flour tortillas
⅓ cup sour cream
½ cup (2 ounces) shredded Cheddar
    cheese

Makes 12 servings

1. Preheat oven to 350°F. Grease 12 muffin pan cups. Set aside.

2. Cook beef and onions in large nonstick skillet until meat is browned; drain. Remove from heat. Stir in tomato sauce, olives, ¼ *cup water*, taco seasoning, **Frank's RedHot** Sauce and egg; mix well.

3. Using 4-inch cookie cutter, cut each flour tortilla into 3 rounds. Fit tortilla rounds into prepared muffin cups. Fill each tortilla cup with ¼ cup meat mixture. Top each with sour cream and cheese.

4. Bake 25 minutes or until heated through.

Vegetable Hummus

Prep Time: 10 minutes   Chill Time: 2 hours

2 cloves garlic
2 cans (15 to 19 ounces each)
    chick peas, rinsed and drained
1 package KNORR® Recipe
    Classics™ Vegetable recipe mix
½ cup water
½ cup BERTOLLI® Olive Oil
2 tablespoons lemon juice
¼ teaspoon ground cumin
6 (8-inch) whole wheat or white pita
    breads, cut into wedges

Makes 3½ cups dip

• In food processor, pulse garlic until finely chopped. Add remaining ingredients except pita. Process until smooth; chill at least 2 hours.

• Stir hummus before serving. If desired, add 1 to 2 tablespoons additional olive oil, or to taste. Serve with pita wedges.

Mini Taco Quiches

Hidden Valley®
Salsa Ranch Dip

1 container (16 ounces) sour cream
  (2 cups)
1 packet (1 ounce) HIDDEN VALLEY®
  The Original Ranch® Dips Mix
½ cup thick and chunky salsa
  Chopped tomatoes and diced
  green chiles (optional)
Tortilla chips, for dipping

Makes 2½ cups dip

Combine sour cream and dips mix. Stir in salsa. Add tomatoes and chiles, if desired. Chill 1 hour. Serve with tortilla chips.

Sausage Cheese Puffs

1 pound BOB EVANS® Original
  Recipe Roll Sausage
2½ cups (10 ounces) shredded
  sharp Cheddar cheese
2 cups biscuit mix
½ cup water
1 teaspoon baking powder

Makes about 60 appetizers

Preheat oven to 350°F. Combine ingredients in large bowl until blended. Shape into 1-inch balls. Place on lightly greased baking sheets. Bake about 25 minutes or until golden brown. Serve hot. Refrigerate leftovers.

Hidden Valley® Salsa Ranch Dip

Hearty Nachos

Prep Time: 10 minutes   Cook Time: 12 minutes

1 pound ground beef
1 envelope LIPTON® RECIPE
    SECRETS® Onion Soup Mix
1 can (19 ounces) black beans,
    rinsed and drained
1 cup prepared salsa
1 package (8½ ounces) plain tortilla
    chips
1 cup shredded Cheddar cheese
    (about 4 ounces)

Makes 8 servings

1. In 12-inch nonstick skillet, brown ground beef over medium-high heat; drain.

2. Stir in soup mix, black beans and salsa. Bring to a boil over high heat. Reduce heat to low and simmer 5 minutes or until heated through.

3. Arrange tortilla chips on serving platter. Spread beef mixture over chips; sprinkle with Cheddar cheese. Top, if desired, with sliced green onions, sliced pitted ripe olives, chopped tomato and chopped cilantro.

Melted Brie & Artichoke Dip

Prep Time: 10 minutes   Cook Time: 30 minutes

1 envelope KNORR® Recipe
    Classics™ Spring Vegetable
    recipe mix
1 can (14 ounces) artichoke hearts,
    drained and chopped
1 cup HELLMANN'S® or BEST
    FOODS® Real Mayonnaise
1 container (8 ounces) sour cream
8 ounces Brie cheese, rind removed
    and cut into chunks

Makes 3 cups dip

Preheat oven to 350°F. In 1-quart casserole, combine all ingredients.

Bake uncovered 30 minutes or until heated through.

Serve with sliced French bread or your favorite dippers.

Hearty Nachos

Potato Skins

4 baked potatoes, quartered
¼ cup sour cream
1 packet (1 ounce) HIDDEN VALLEY®
    The Original Ranch® Salad
    Dressing & Seasoning Mix
1 cup (4 ounces) shredded Cheddar
    cheese
    Sliced green onions and/or bacon
    pieces* (optional)

*Crisp-cooked, crumbled bacon can
be used.

Makes 8 to 10 servings

Scoop potato out of skins; combine potatoes, sour cream
and salad dressing & seasoning mix in medium bowl. Fill
skins with potato mixture. Sprinkle with cheese. Bake
at 375°F for 12 to 15 minutes or until cheese is melted.
Garnish with green onions and/or bacon bits, if desired.

Ranch Drummettes

½ cup butter or margarine
¼ cup hot pepper sauce
3 tablespoons vinegar
24 chicken wing drummettes
1 packet (1 ounce) HIDDEN VALLEY®
    The Original Ranch® Salad
    Dressing & Seasoning Mix
½ teaspoon paprika
    Additional HIDDEN VALLEY® The
    Original Ranch® Salad Dressing
    Celery sticks (optional)

Makes 6 to 8 servings (or 24 drummettes)

Melt butter and whisk together with pepper sauce and
vinegar in a small bowl. Dip drummettes in butter mixture;
arrange in a single layer in a large baking pan. Sprinkle
with salad dressing & seasoning mix. Bake at 350°F for
30 to 40 minutes or until juices run clear and chicken is
browned. Sprinkle with paprika. Serve with additional
prepared salad dressing and celery sticks, if desired.

Top to bottom: Potato Skins and Ranch Drummettes

Home-Style Corn Cakes

1 cup yellow cornmeal
½ cup all-purpose flour
½ teaspoon baking powder
½ teaspoon baking soda
1 envelope LIPTON® RECIPE
SECRETS® Onion Soup Mix*
¾ cup buttermilk
1 egg, beaten
1 can (14¾ ounces) cream-style corn
2 ounces roasted red peppers,
chopped (about ¼ cup)
I CAN'T BELIEVE IT'S NOT
BUTTER!® Spread

*Or, substitute Lipton® RECIPE SECRETS®
Golden Onion Soup Mix.

Makes about 18 corn cakes

1. In large bowl, combine cornmeal, flour, baking powder and baking soda. Blend soup mix with buttermilk, egg, corn and roasted red peppers; stir into cornmeal mixture.

2. In 12-inch nonstick skillet or on griddle, melt ½ teaspoon Spread over medium heat. Drop ¼ cup batter for each corn cake and cook, turning once, 5 minutes or until cooked through and golden brown. Remove to serving platter and keep warm. Repeat with remaining batter and additional I Can't Believe It's Not Butter!® Spread if needed. Serve with sour cream and salsa, if desired.

quick tip

Leftover corn cakes may be wrapped and frozen. Remove from the wrapping and reheat straight from the freezer in a preheated 350°F oven for 15 minutes or until heated through.

Home-Style Corn Cakes

Hidden Valley® Torta

2 packages (8 ounces each) cream cheese, softened
1 packet (1 ounce) HIDDEN VALLEY® The Original Ranch® Salad Dressing & Seasoning Mix
1 jar (6 ounces) marinated artichoke hearts, drained and chopped
⅓ cup roasted red peppers, drained and chopped
3 tablespoons minced fresh parsley

Makes 10 to 12 servings

Combine cream cheese and salad dressing & seasoning mix in a medium bowl. In a separate bowl, combine artichokes, peppers and parsley. In a 3-cup bowl lined with plastic wrap, alternate layers of cream cheese mixture and vegetable mixture, beginning and ending with a cheese layer.

Chill 4 hours or overnight. Invert onto plate; remove plastic wrap. Serve with crackers.

Fiesta Party Mix

Prep Time: 10 minutes   Cook Time: 40 minutes

1 package LAWRY'S® Chili Spices & Seasonings
½ cup I CAN'T BELIEVE IT'S NOT BUTTER!® Spread,* melted
2 cups crispy wheat squares cereal
2 cups crispy corn squares cereal
1 box (10 ounces) bite-size cheese crackers
1 can (10 ounces to 11.5 ounces) mixed nuts
1 cup small twist pretzels

Do not use tub products.

Makes about 12 cups

Preheat oven to 300°F.

In large bowl, combine all ingredients. In large roasting pan, evenly spread mixture. Bake, stirring once, 40 minutes. Serve warm or cool completely and store in airtight container until ready to serve.

Hidden Valley® Torta

7-Layer Ranch Dip

Prep Time: 15 minutes

1 envelope LIPTON® RECIPE
    SECRETS® Ranch Soup Mix
1 container (16 ounces) sour cream
1 cup shredded lettuce
1 medium tomato, chopped
    (about 1 cup)
1 can (2.25 ounces) sliced pitted ripe
    olives, drained
¼ cup chopped red onion
1 can (4.5 ounces) chopped green
    chilies, drained
1 cup shredded Cheddar cheese
    (about 4 ounces)

Makes 7 cups dip

1. In 2-quart shallow dish, combine soup mix and sour cream.

2. Evenly layer remaining ingredients, ending with cheese. Chill, if desired. Serve with tortilla chips.

Pecan Cheese Ball

Prep Time: 15 minutes   Chill Time: 1 hour

2 packages (8 ounces each) cream
    cheese, softened
1 package shredded Cheddar
    cheese (about 8 ounces)
1 envelope LIPTON® RECIPE
    SECRETS® Onion Soup Mix
2 tablespoons finely chopped fresh
    parsley
½ teaspoon garlic powder
½ cup finely chopped pecans,
    toasted if desired

Makes 1 cheese ball

1. In large bowl, with electric mixer, beat cream cheese until light and fluffy, about 2 minutes. Stir in Cheddar cheese, soup mix, parsley and garlic powder.

2. Wet hands with cold water. Roll cheese mixture into ball. Roll cheese ball in pecans until evenly coated.

3. Refrigerate 1 hour or until set. Serve with crackers.

7-Layer Ranch Dip

Quick Hot and Sour Chicken Soup (*page 32*)

hurry-up
soups & stews

1 pound beef stew meat
1 can (10¾ ounces) condensed
    cream of mushroom soup,
    undiluted
2 cans (4 ounces each) sliced
    mushrooms, drained
1 package (1 ounce) dry onion
    soup mix
  Hot cooked noodles

Mushroom-Beef Stew

Makes 4 servings

SLOW COOKER DIRECTIONS

Combine all ingredients except noodles in slow cooker.
Cover; cook on LOW 8 to 10 hours. Serve over noodles.

Quick Hot and Sour Chicken Soup

2 cups chicken broth
2 cups water
1 package (about 10 ounces)
    refrigerated fully cooked
    chicken breast strips, cut
    into pieces
1 package (about 7 ounces)
    reduced-sodium chicken-
    flavored rice and vermicelli mix
1 large jalapeño pepper,* minced
2 green onions, chopped
1 tablespoon soy sauce
1 tablespoon fresh lime juice
1 tablespoon minced fresh cilantro
    (optional)

**Jalapeño peppers can sting and irritate
the skin, so wear rubber gloves when
handling peppers and do not touch
your eyes.*

Makes 4 servings

1. Combine chicken broth, water, chicken, rice mix,
jalapeño pepper, green onions and soy sauce in large
saucepan. Bring to a boil over high heat. Reduce heat to
low. Cover and simmer 20 minutes or until rice is tender,
stirring occasionally.

2. Stir in lime juice; sprinkle with cilantro.

Mushroom-Beef Stew

2 cups water
1 package KNORR® Recipe
Classics™ Vegetable or Spring
Vegetable recipe mix
1 bottle or can (8 to 10 ounces)
clam juice
2 teaspoons tomato paste
½ teaspoon paprika
¼ teaspoon saffron threads (optional)
12 mussels or clams, well scrubbed
1½ pounds mixed seafood (cubed cod,
snapper, scallops or shrimp)

Bouillabaisse

Prep Time: 15 minutes   Cook Time: 10 minutes

Makes 6 servings

• In 3-quart saucepan, bring water, recipe mix, clam juice, tomato paste, paprika and saffron to a boil over medium-high heat, stirring occasionally.

• Add mussels and seafood. Bring to a boil over high heat.

• Reduce heat to low and simmer 5 minutes or until shells open and seafood is cooked through and flakes easily when tested with fork. Discard any unopened shells.

4 thick slices bacon, diced
¾ cup chopped onion
2 cups chicken broth or water
2 cups milk
1 (6.2-ounce) package PASTA
RONI® Shells & White Cheddar
1 cup frozen or canned corn,
drained
½ cup finely diced red bell pepper
¼ cup chopped chives or green
onions

Hearty Corn & Cheese Chowder

Prep Time: 10 minutes   Cook Time: 25 minutes

Makes 4 servings

1. In large saucepan over medium heat, cook bacon 5 minutes. Add onion; cook 5 minutes or until bacon is crisp, stirring occasionally. Remove from saucepan; drain. Set aside.

2. To same saucepan, add chicken broth, milk, pasta, corn and bell pepper; bring to a boil. Reduce heat to medium. Simmer uncovered, 12 minutes or until pasta is tender.

3. Stir in bacon mixture and Special Seasonings. Return to a boil; boil 2 to 3 minutes. Ladle into bowls; top with chives.

Bouillabaisse

2 tablespoons vegetable oil
1 red bell pepper, diced
1 stalk celery, sliced
1 can (about 14 ounces) diced
    tomatoes with roasted garlic
    and onions
1½ cups chicken broth
1 package (about 10 ounces)
    refrigerated fully cooked
    chicken breast strips, cut
    into pieces
1 cup canned kidney beans, rinsed
    and drained
1 pouch (about 9 ounces) New
    Orleans-style chicken-flavored
    ready-to-serve rice mix
¼ teaspoon hot pepper sauce
¼ cup chopped green onions,
    green parts only

Easy Cajun Chicken Stew

Makes 4 servings

1. Heat oil in Dutch oven over medium-high heat. Add bell pepper and celery; cook and stir 3 minutes. Add tomatoes and chicken broth; bring to a boil.

2. Add chicken, beans, rice mix and pepper sauce. Reduce heat to low. Cover; cook 7 minutes. Stir in green onions. Remove from heat. Cover; let stand 2 to 3 minutes to thicken.

Tip: If canned diced tomatoes with roasted garlic and onions aren't available, substitute 1 can (about 14 ounces) diced tomatoes; add 1 teaspoon minced garlic and ¼ cup chopped onions to the bell pepper mixture.

1 package KNORR® Recipe
    Classics™ Tomato with
    Basil recipe mix
4 cups water
2 cups sliced fennel or broccoli
    florets
1 large zucchini, diced
    (about 2 cups)
1 teaspoon dried oregano
    Grated Parmesan cheese (optional)

Italian Vegetable Soup
Prep Time: 20 minutes   Cook Time: 25 minutes

Makes 6 (1-cup) servings

• In 4-quart Dutch oven, combine recipe mix, water, fennel, zucchini and oregano. Bring to a boil over medium-high heat, stirring occasionally.

• Reduce heat, cover and simmer 15 minutes or until vegetables are tender, stirring occasionally.

• Sprinkle lightly with Parmesan cheese, if desired.

Easy Cajun Chicken Stew

¼ cup chopped onion
3 tablespoons butter or margarine
½ pound fresh mushrooms, sliced
2 tablespoons Worcestershire sauce
1½ cups half-and-half
1 can (10¾ ounces) condensed
    cream of potato soup, undiluted
¼ cup dry white wine
1 packet (1 ounce) HIDDEN VALLEY®
    The Original Ranch® Salad
    Dressing & Seasoning Mix
1 can (10 ounces) whole baby
    clams, undrained
    Chopped fresh parsley

Ranch Clam Chowder

Makes 6 servings

In a 3-quart saucepan, cook onion in butter over medium heat until onion is soft but not browned. Add mushrooms and Worcestershire sauce. Cook until mushrooms are soft and pan juices have almost evaporated. In a medium bowl, whisk together half-and-half, potato soup, wine and salad dressing & seasoning mix until smooth. Drain clam liquid into dressing mixture; stir into mushrooms in pan. Cook, uncovered, until soup is heated through but not boiling. Add clams to soup; cook until heated through. Garnish each serving with parsley.

1 can (10¾ ounces) condensed
    cream of roasted chicken soup
    with savory herbs, undiluted
1 bag (16 ounces) frozen
    Southwestern or Mexican-style
    vegetables
1 package (10 ounces) PERDUE®
    SHORT CUTS® Fully Cooked
    Carved Chicken Breast,
    Honey Roasted
1 package (8 ounces) shredded
    Mexican cheese or Monterey
    Jack cheese (2 cups), divided
1½ cups buttermilk baking mix
½ cup milk

Quick Chicken Stew with Biscuits

Prep Time: 10 minutes   Cook Time: 35 to 40 minutes

Makes 4 to 6 servings

Preheat oven to 425°F. In lightly greased 12×8-inch baking dish, combine soup and ½ soup can water. Stir in frozen vegetables, chicken and 1 cup cheese. Cover and bake 20 minutes. Meanwhile, in mixing bowl, combine baking mix, remaining 1 cup cheese and milk; stir with fork until all of baking mix is moistened. Spoon baking mix on top of chicken mixture. Bake 15 to 20 minutes, until biscuit topping is golden brown and sauce is hot and bubbly.

Ranch Clam Chowder

Southwestern Beef Stew

1 tablespoon plus 1 teaspoon
   BERTOLLI® Olive Oil, divided
1½ pounds boneless beef chuck,
   cut into 1-inch cubes
1 can (4 ounces) chopped green
   chilies, drained
2 cloves garlic, finely chopped
1 teaspoon ground cumin (optional)
1 can (14 to 16 ounces) whole or
   plum tomatoes, undrained
   and chopped
1 envelope LIPTON® RECIPE
   SECRETS® Onion or Beefy
   Onion Soup Mix
1 cup water
1 package (10 ounces) frozen cut
   okra or green beans, thawed
1 large red or green bell pepper,
   cut into 1-inch pieces
4 frozen half-ears corn on the cob,
   thawed and each cut into
   3 round pieces
2 tablespoons chopped fresh cilantro
   (optional)

Makes 6 servings

1. In 5-quart Dutch oven or heavy saucepan, heat 1 tablespoon oil over medium-high heat and brown half of beef; remove and set aside. Repeat with remaining beef; remove and set aside.

2. In same Dutch oven, heat remaining 1 teaspoon oil over medium heat and cook chilies, garlic and cumin, stirring constantly, for 3 minutes. Return beef to Dutch oven. Stir in tomatoes and soup mix blended with water. Bring to a boil over high heat. Reduce heat to low and simmer covered, stirring occasionally, for 1 hour.

3. Stir in okra, red pepper and corn. Bring to a boil over high heat. Reduce heat to low and simmer covered, stirring occasionally, for 30 minutes or until meat is tender. Sprinkle with cilantro.

quick tip

Canned tomotoes can be chopped right in the can—just snip them into pieces with a kitchen scissors. It's quick and easy and a lot less messy than transferring the tomatoes to a cutting board to do the job.

Southwestern Beef Stew

Thai Noodle Soup

Prep and Cook Time: 15 minutes

1 package (3 ounces) ramen noodles
¾ pound chicken tenders
2 cans (about 14 ounces each)
    chicken broth
¼ cup shredded carrot
¼ cup frozen snow peas
2 tablespoons thinly sliced green
    onions
½ teaspoon minced garlic
¼ teaspoon ground ginger
3 tablespoons chopped fresh cilantro
½ lime, cut into 4 wedges

Makes 4 servings

1. Break noodles into pieces. Cook noodles according to package directions; discard flavor packet. Drain and set aside.

2. Cut chicken into ½-inch pieces. Combine chicken broth and chicken in large saucepan or Dutch oven; bring to a boil over medium heat. Cook 2 minutes.

3. Add carrot, snow peas, green onions, garlic and ginger. Reduce heat to low; simmer 3 minutes. Stir in cooked noodles and cilantro; heat through. Serve soup with lime wedges.

Creamy Leek Chowder

Prep Time: 10 minutes   Cook Time: 10 minutes

1 package (1.8 ounces) leek
    soup mix
2¼ cups water
1½ cups milk
1 can (14.5 ounces) whole new
    potatoes, drained and cut
    into small cubes
1⅓ cups **French's**® French Fried
    Onions, divided
2 teaspoons chopped fresh thyme *or*
    ½ teaspoon dried thyme leaves
¼ teaspoon ground black pepper
    Sour cream
    Chopped parsley

Makes 4 servings

1. Combine soup mix, water and milk in large saucepan; whisk until well blended. Stir in potatoes, *1 cup* French Fried Onions, thyme and pepper. Bring to a boil over medium-high heat. Reduce heat to low. Simmer, uncovered, 10 minutes, stirring occasionally.

2. Ladle into individual bowls. Top with sour cream, parsley and remaining ⅓ *cup* onions.

Tip: To crisp and brown French Fried Onions, place on paper towels and microwave on HIGH 1 minute.

Thai Noodle Soup

Country Chicken Stew with Dumplings

1 tablespoon BERTOLLI® Olive Oil
1 (3- to 3½-pound) chicken, cut into
    serving pieces (with or without
    skin)
4 large carrots, cut into 2-inch pieces
3 ribs celery, cut into 1-inch pieces
1 large onion, cut into 1-inch
    wedges
1 envelope LIPTON® RECIPE
    SECRETS® Savory Herb
    with Garlic Soup Mix*
1½ cups water
½ cup apple juice
    Parsley Dumplings (optional,
    recipe follows)

*Also terrific with LIPTON® RECIPE
SECRETS® Golden Onion Soup Mix.*

Makes about 6 servings

1. In 6-quart Dutch oven or heavy saucepan, heat oil over medium-high heat and brown half of the chicken; remove and set aside. Repeat with remaining chicken. Return chicken to Dutch oven. Stir in carrots, celery, onion, soup mix blended with water and apple juice. Bring to a boil over high heat. Reduce heat to low; simmer, covered, 25 minutes or until chicken is thoroughly cooked, juices run clear and vegetables are tender.

2. Meanwhile, prepare Parsley Dumplings. Drop 12 rounded tablespoonfuls of batter into simmering broth around chicken. Continue simmering, covered, 10 minutes or until toothpick inserted into center of dumplings comes out clean. Season stew, if desired, with salt and black pepper.

Parsley Dumplings: In medium bowl, combine 1⅓ cups all-purpose flour, 2 teaspoons baking powder, 1 tablespoon chopped fresh parsley and ½ teaspoon salt; set aside. In measuring cup, blend ⅔ cup milk, 2 tablespoons melted butter or margarine and 1 egg. Stir milk mixture into flour mixture just until blended.

Variation: Add 1 pound quartered red potatoes to stew with carrots; omit dumplings.

Country Chicken Stew with Dumplings

Patrick's Irish Lamb Soup

1 tablespoon olive oil
1 medium onion, coarsely chopped
1½ pounds fresh lean American lamb
    boneless shoulder, cut into
    ¾-inch cubes
1 bottle (12 ounces) beer *or* ¾ cup
    water
1 teaspoon seasoned pepper
2 cans (14½ ounces each) beef
    broth
1 package (about 1 ounce) brown
    gravy mix
3 cups cubed potatoes
2 cups thinly sliced carrots
2 cups shredded green cabbage
⅓ cup chopped fresh parsley
    (optional)

Makes 8 servings

In 3-quart saucepan with cover, heat oil. Add onion and sauté until brown, stirring occasionally. Add lamb and cook and stir until browned. Stir in beer and pepper. Cover and simmer 30 minutes.

Stir in broth and gravy mix. Add potatoes and carrots; cover and simmer 15 to 20 minutes or until vegetables are tender. Stir in cabbage and cook just until cabbage turns bright green. Garnish with chopped parsley, if desired.

*Favorite recipe from **American Lamb Council***

Cheese Ravioli Soup

Preparation Time: 5 minutes   Cooking Time: 20 minutes

4 cans (20 ounces each) chicken
    broth
1 package (16 ounces) frozen red
    pepper stir-fry
4 tablespoons MRS. DASH® Classic
    Italiano Blend
1 package (13 ounces) frozen mini
    cheese ravioli
6 tablespoons grated Parmesan
    cheese

Makes 12 servings

Combine broth, red pepper stir-fry and Classic Italiano Blend in medium saucepan. Bring to a boil. Add ravioli. Simmer 15 to 20 minutes or until ravioli is done. Serve garnished with grated Parmesan cheese.

Patrick's Irish Lamb Soup

Chicken and Wild Rice Soup

Prep Time: 20 minutes   Cook Time: 6 to 7 hours

3 cans (14½ ounces each) chicken broth
1 pound boneless skinless chicken breasts or thighs, cut into bite-size pieces
2 cups water
1 cup sliced celery
1 cup diced carrots
1 package (6 ounces) converted long grain and wild rice mix with seasoning packet (not quick-cooking or instant rice)
½ cup chopped onion
½ teaspoon black pepper
2 teaspoons white vinegar (optional)
1 tablespoon dried parsley flakes

Makes 9 (1½-cup) servings

SLOW COOKER DIRECTIONS

1. Combine chicken broth, chicken, water, celery, carrots, rice and seasoning packet, onion and pepper in slow cooker; mix well.

2. Cover; cook on LOW 6 to 7 hours or on HIGH 4 to 5 hours or until chicken is tender.

3. Stir in vinegar, if desired. Sprinkle with parsley.

Meatball & Pasta Soup

Prep Time: 10 minutes   Cook Time: 15 minutes

2 cans (14½ ounces each) chicken broth
4 cups water
1 can (15 ounces) crushed tomatoes
1 package (15 ounces) frozen precooked Italian style meatballs, not in sauce
1 envelope LIPTON® RECIPE SECRETS® Onion Soup Mix
½ teaspoon garlic powder
1 cup uncooked mini pasta (such as conchigliette or ditalini)
4 cups fresh baby spinach leaves

Makes 8 servings

1. In 6-quart saucepan, bring broth, water, crushed tomatoes, meatballs, soup mix and garlic powder to a boil over medium-high heat.

2. Add pasta and cook 5 minutes or until pasta is almost tender. Stir in spinach. Reduce heat to medium and simmer uncovered 2 minutes or until spinach is wilted and pasta is tender. Serve, if desired, with Parmesan cheese.

Tip: For a real flavor boost, try using LIPTON® RECIPE SECRETS® Soup Mix as a dry rub; try it on chicken, steak, pork or vegetables.

Chicken and Wild Rice Soup

Southwestern Turkey Stew

1 tablespoon vegetable oil
1 small onion, finely chopped
1 clove garlic, minced
2 cups reduced-sodium chicken
    broth
2 cups cooked smoked turkey breast,
    cut into ½-inch pieces
2 cups frozen corn kernels
1 can (about 14 ounces) diced
    tomatoes
1 package (about 6 ounces) red
    beans and rice mix
1 to 2 canned chipotle peppers in
    adobo sauce,* drained and
    minced
    Chopped green onion (optional)

*Canned chipotle peppers can be found in the Mexican section of most supermarkets or gourmet food stores. Chipotle peppers can sting and irritate the skin, so wear rubber gloves when handling peppers and do not touch your eyes.

Makes 4 servings

1. Heat oil in large nonstick skillet over medium-high heat. Add onion and garlic; cook and stir 3 minutes or until onion is translucent.

2. Add chicken broth; bring to a boil. Stir in turkey, corn, tomatoes, bean mix and chipotle pepper. Reduce heat to low. Cover; cook 10 to 12 minutes or until rice is tender. Let stand 3 minutes. Garnish with green onion.

Substitutions: Use 1 can (about 14 ounces) diced tomatoes with jalapeño peppers *or* ¼ teaspoon chipotle chili powder and 1 minced jalapeño pepper in place of the chipotle pepper.

quick tip

Chipotle peppers are smoked jalapeños. They are usually found canned with adobo sauce, which is a dark red Mexican-style sauce made of chili peppers, herbs and vinegar. If you have leftover chipotle peppers from the can you open for a recipe, they can easily be frozen with the adobo sauce in a food-safe container for later use.

Southwestern Turkey Stew

2 tablespoons all-purpose flour
2 teaspoons blackened seasoning
mix or Creole seasoning mix
¾ pound boneless skinless chicken
thighs, cut into ¾-inch pieces
2 teaspoons olive oil
1 large onion, coarsely chopped
½ cup sliced celery
2 teaspoons minced garlic
1 can (about 14 ounces) reduced-
sodium chicken broth
1 can (14½ ounces) no-salt-added
stewed tomatoes, undrained
1 large green bell pepper, cut into
chunks
1 teaspoon filé powder (optional)
2 cups hot cooked rice
2 tablespoons chopped fresh parsley

Chicken Gumbo

Prep Time: 15 minutes   Cook Time: 40 minutes

Makes 4 servings

1. Combine flour and blackened seasoning mix in large resealable food storage bag. Add chicken; toss to coat. Heat oil in large deep nonstick skillet or saucepan over medium heat. Add chicken to skillet; sprinkle with any remaining flour mixture. Cook and stir 3 minutes. Add onion, celery and garlic; cook and stir 3 minutes.

2. Add chicken broth, tomatoes with juice and bell pepper; bring to a boil. Reduce heat; cover and simmer 20 minutes or until vegetables are tender. Uncover; simmer 5 to 10 minutes or until sauce is slightly reduced. Remove from heat; stir in filé powder, if desired. Ladle into shallow bowls; top with rice and parsley.

Note: Filé powder, made from dried sassafras leaves, thickens and adds flavor to gumbos. Look for it in the herb and spice section of your supermarket.

1 can (14½ ounces) chicken broth
1 cup milk
¾ cup plain lowfat yogurt
¼ cup mayonnaise
1 packet (1 ounce) HIDDEN VALLEY®
The Original Ranch® Salad
Dressing & Seasoning Mix
1 large ripe avocado, cut into chunks
1 medium tomato, diced
½ unpared cucumber, seeded, diced
¼ cup finely diced purple onion
Avocado slices

Avocado Ranch Soup

Makes 6 servings

In a blender, combine chicken broth, milk, yogurt, mayonnaise, salad dressing & seasoning mix and avocado chunks. Purée until smooth. Pour mixture into large bowl. Stir in tomato, cucumber and onion. Cover and refrigerate at least 4 hours. Garnish each bowl with avocado slices before serving.

Chicken Gumbo

Oven-Baked Stew

Prep Time: 20 minutes   Cook Time: 2 hours

2 pounds boneless beef chuck or
round steak, cut into 1-inch
cubes
¼ cup all-purpose flour
1⅓ cups sliced carrots
1 can (14 to 16 ounces) whole
peeled tomatoes, undrained
and chopped
1 envelope LIPTON® RECIPE
SECRETS® Onion Soup Mix*
½ cup dry red wine or water
1 cup fresh or canned sliced
mushrooms
1 package (8 ounces) medium or
broad egg noodles, cooked
and drained

*Also terrific with LIPTON® RECIPE
SECRETS® Beefy Onion or Onion
Mushroom Soup Mix.*

Makes 8 servings

1. Preheat oven to 425°F. In 2½-quart shallow casserole,
toss beef with flour, then bake uncovered 20 minutes,
stirring once.

2. *Reduce heat to 350°F.* Stir in carrots, tomatoes, soup
mix and wine.

3. Bake covered 1½ hours or until beef is tender. Stir in
mushrooms and bake covered an additional 10 minutes.
Serve over hot noodles.

Slow Cooker Method: In slow cooker, toss beef with
flour. Add carrots, tomatoes, soup mix and wine. Cook
covered on LOW 8 to 10 hours. Add mushrooms; cook
covered on LOW 30 minutes or until beef is tender. Serve
over hot noodles.

Mexicali Vegetable Soup

½ pound ground beef
½ cup chopped onion
3½ cups (two 15-ounce cans)
beef broth
1 can (14½ ounces) small white
beans, drained
1 cup sliced zucchini
1 cup frozen sliced carrots
1 package (1.25 ounces) ORTEGA®
Taco Seasoning Mix

Makes 6 to 8 servings

COOK beef and onion in large saucepan until beef is
browned; drain. Add broth, beans, zucchini, carrots
and seasoning mix. Bring to a boil. Reduce heat to
low; cook, covered, for 15 to 20 minutes.

Oven-Baked Stew

California Crab Salad *(page 58)*

super speedy
salads

Crunchy Layered Beef & Bean Salad

Prep Time: 10 minutes   Cook Time: 6 minutes

1 pound ground beef or turkey
2 cans (15 to 19 ounces each) black beans or pinto beans, rinsed and drained
1 can (14½ ounces) stewed tomatoes, undrained
1⅓ cups **French's**® French Fried Onions, divided
1 tablespoon **Frank's**® **RedHot**® Original Cayenne Pepper Sauce
1 package (1¼ ounces) taco seasoning mix
6 cups shredded lettuce
1 cup (4 ounces) shredded Cheddar or Monterey Jack cheese

Makes 6 servings

1. Cook beef in large nonstick skillet over medium heat until thoroughly browned; drain well. Stir in beans, tomatoes, ⅔ *cup* French Fried Onions, **Frank's RedHot** Sauce and taco seasoning. Heat to boiling. Cook over medium heat 5 minutes, stirring occasionally.

2. Spoon beef mixture over lettuce on serving platter. Top with cheese.

3. Microwave remaining ⅔ *cup* onions 1 minute on HIGH. Sprinkle over salad.

California Crab Salad

1 packet (0.4 ounce) HIDDEN VALLEY® The Original Ranch® Buttermilk Recipe Salad Dressing Mix
1 cup buttermilk
1 cup mayonnaise
1 tablespoon grated fresh ginger
1 teaspoon prepared horseradish
2 cups cooked white rice, chilled
4 lettuce leaves
8 ounces cooked crabmeat, chilled
1 large ripe avocado, thinly sliced
½ medium cucumber, thinly sliced

Makes 4 servings

In a medium bowl, whisk together salad dressing mix, buttermilk and mayonnaise. Whisk in ginger and horseradish. Cover and refrigerate 30 minutes. To serve, arrange ½ cup rice on top of each lettuce leaf. Top with 2 tablespoons of the dressing. Arrange one-quarter of the crabmeat, avocado and cucumber on top of each rice mound. Serve with remaining dressing. Garnish with cherry tomatoes and lime wedges, if desired.

Crunchy Layered Beef & Bean Salad

1 (6.8-ounce) package
RICE-A-RONI® Beef Flavor
2 tablespoons margarine or butter
8 ounces thick sliced deli roast beef,
cut into ½-inch pieces
½ cup chopped red onion
½ cup sliced ripe olives
3 plum tomatoes, seeded and
chopped
⅓ cup olive oil
¼ cup lemon juice
2 cloves garlic, crushed
½ teaspoon dried oregano
½ teaspoon ground black pepper
1 medium cucumber, thinly sliced
½ cup (2 ounces) crumbled feta
cheese

Greek Isle Rice Salad

Prep Time: 15 minutes   Cook Time: 30 minutes

Makes 6 servings

1. In large skillet over medium heat, sauté rice-vermicelli mix with margarine until vermicelli is golden brown.

2. Slowly stir in 2½ cups water and Special Seasonings; bring to a boil. Reduce heat to low. Simmer 15 to 20 minutes or until rice is tender. Cool completely.

3. In large bowl, combine rice mixture, roast beef, onion, olives and tomatoes; set aside.

4. In small bowl, combine olive oil, lemon juice, garlic, oregano and pepper with wire whisk. Toss rice mixture with dressing. Chill at least 30 minutes. Garnish with cucumber slices and cheese.

Pineapple Chicken Salad

1 packet (1 ounce) HIDDEN VALLEY®
The Original Ranch® Salad
Dressing & Seasoning Mix
½ cup mayonnaise
¼ cup pineapple juice
2 cups cubed cooked chicken
1 cup sliced celery
1 can (20 ounces) pineapple chunks
(reserve juice for above)

Makes 4 to 6 servings

Combine salad dressing & seasoning mix with mayonnaise and pineapple juice. Add chicken, celery and pineapple to mixture and toss well to coat. Chill.

Greek Isle Rice Salad

1 package KNORR® Recipe
Classics™ Tomato with
Basil recipe mix
½ cup BERTOLLI® Classico™ Olive Oil
½ cup red wine vinegar
1 package (16 ounces) frozen
tortellini, cooked and drained
(reserve ¼ cup pasta water)
3 cups day-old or toasted bread
cubes
1 cup sliced pepperoni (4 ounces)
4 ounces provolone cheese, cut into
½-inch cubes (about 1 cup)
⅓ cup pitted Kalamata olives, sliced
¼ cup thinly sliced red onion

Panzanella
Prep Time: 20 minutes   Chill Time: 2 hours

Makes 6 servings

In large bowl, combine recipe mix, olive oil, vinegar and reserved pasta water. Add remaining ingredients; toss to coat. Chill 2 hours.

1 package (6.25 ounces)
quick-cooking long grain
and wild rice mix
1 bag (16 ounces) BIRDS EYE®
frozen Cauliflower, Carrots
and Pea Pods
⅓ cup honey Dijon or favorite salad
dressing
2 green onions, thinly sliced
¼ cup sliced almonds

Wild Rice and Vegetable Salad
Prep Time: 5 minutes   Cook Time: 15 minutes

Makes about 4 side-dish servings

• Cook rice according to package directions. Transfer to large bowl.

• Cook vegetables according to package directions. Drain; add to rice.

• Stir in dressing, green onions and almonds.

• Serve warm or cover and chill until ready to serve.

Serving Suggestion: Use this recipe as the base for a variety of main-dish salads, adding smoked chicken or turkey or cooked seafood to the rice and vegetables.

Panzanella

Tex-Mex Flank Steak Salad

½ beef flank steak (about 6 ounces)
½ teaspoon Mexican seasoning
    blend or chili powder
⅛ teaspoon salt
    Olive oil cooking spray
4 cups packaged mixed salad
    greens
1 can (11 ounces) mandarin orange
    sections, drained
2 tablespoons green taco sauce

Makes 2 servings

1. Cut flank steak lengthwise in half, then crosswise into thin strips. Combine steak, Mexican seasoning and salt in medium bowl.

2. Lightly spray large skillet with cooking spray. Heat over medium-high heat. Add steak; cook and stir 1 to 2 minutes or to desired doneness.

3. Toss together greens and orange sections. Arrange on serving plates. Top with warm steak; drizzle with taco sauce.

Grilled Potato Salad

1 envelope LIPTON® RECIPE
    SECRETS® Onion Soup Mix*
⅓ cup BERTOLLI® Olive Oil
2 tablespoons red wine vinegar
1 clove garlic, finely chopped
2 pounds small red or all-purpose
    potatoes, cut into 1-inch cubes
1 tablespoon chopped fresh basil
    leaves *or* 1 teaspoon dried
    basil leaves, crushed
    Freshly ground black pepper

*Also terrific with LIPTON® RECIPE SECRETS® Onion Mushroom or Golden Onion Soup Mix.

Makes 4 servings

1. In large bowl, blend soup mix, oil, vinegar and garlic; stir in potatoes.

2. Grease 30×18-inch sheet of heavy-duty aluminum foil; top with potato mixture. Wrap foil loosely around mixture, sealing edges airtight with double fold. Place on another sheet of 30×18-inch foil; seal edges airtight with double fold in opposite direction.

3. Grill, shaking package occasionally and turning package once, 40 minutes or until potatoes are tender. Spoon into serving bowl and toss with basil and pepper. Serve slightly warm or at room temperature.

Oven Method: Preheat oven to 450°F. Prepare foil packet as above. Place in large baking pan on bottom rack and bake, turning packet once, 40 minutes or until potatoes are tender. Toss and serve as above.

Tex-Mex Flank Steak Salad

Hidden Valley®
Chopstick Chicken Salad

1 packet (1 ounce) HIDDEN VALLEY®
    The Original Ranch® Salad
    Dressing & Seasoning Mix
1 cup milk
1 cup mayonnaise
2 tablespoons soy sauce
8 cups torn lettuce
2 cups shredded cooked chicken
1 cup chopped green onions
1 cup chopped water chestnuts
1 cup toasted sliced almonds
    (optional)

Makes 4 to 6 servings

In a bowl, combine salad dressing & seasoning mix with milk and mayonnaise. Mix well. Cover and refrigerate. Chill 30 minutes to thicken. Stir in soy sauce. Toss with lettuce, chicken, onions and water chestnuts; top with almonds, if desired.

Note: To make Lower Fat Hidden Valley® The Original Ranch® Salad Dressing & Seasoning Mix, substitute low-fat milk and light mayonnaise for regular milk and mayonnaise.

Chicken, Cherry and
Wild Rice Salad

DRESSING
¼ cup olive oil
3 tablespoons soy sauce
3 tablespoons lemon juice
1½ teaspoons ground ginger
⅛ teaspoon black pepper

SALAD
1 (6-ounce) package long grain
    wild rice mix
2 cups cubed cooked chicken
1 cup snow pea pods, cut crosswise
    in half and cooked
½ cup dried tart cherries

Makes 4 servings

For dressing, combine olive oil, soy sauce, lemon juice, ginger and pepper; mix well.

For salad, prepare rice according to package directions. Meanwhile, combine chicken, snow peas and cherries. Pour dressing over chicken mixture; mix well. Let rice cool about 15 minutes. Stir rice into chicken mixture. Refrigerate, covered, at least 1 hour before serving.

Favorite recipe from **Cherry Marketing Institute**

Hidden Valley® Chopstick Chicken Salad

Asian Shrimp & Noodle Salad

Prep Time: 15 minutes   Cook Time: 10 minutes

⅓ cup plus 2 tablespoons vegetable oil, divided
¼ cup cider vinegar
2 tablespoons **French's®** Worcestershire Sauce
2 tablespoons light soy sauce
2 tablespoons honey
1 teaspoon grated fresh ginger *or* ¼ teaspoon ground ginger
2 packages (3 ounces each) chicken-flavor ramen noodle soup
1 pound shrimp, cleaned and deveined with tails left on
2 cups vegetables such as broccoli, carrots and snow peas, cut into bite-size pieces
1⅓ cups **French's®** French Fried Onions, divided

Makes 6 servings

1. Combine ⅓ cup oil, vinegar, Worcestershire, soy sauce, honey and ginger until well blended; set aside. Prepare ramen noodles according to package directions for soup; drain and rinse noodles. Place in large serving bowl.

2. Stir-fry shrimp in 1 tablespoon oil in large skillet over medium-high heat, stirring constantly, until shrimp turn pink. Remove shrimp to bowl with noodles. Stir-fry vegetables in remaining 1 tablespoon oil in skillet over medium-high heat, stirring constantly, until vegetables are crisp-tender.

3. Add vegetable mixture, dressing and *1 cup* French Fried Onions to bowl with noodles; toss to coat well. Serve immediately topped with remaining ⅓ *cup* onions.

Tip: Purchase cut-up vegetables from the salad bar at your local supermarket to save prep time.

quick tip

To devein shrimp, cut a shallow slit along the back of the shrimp with a paring knife, then lift out the vein. (You may find this easier to do under cold running water.) The veins of large and jumbo shrimp are gritty; they must always be removed.

Asian Shrimp & Noodle Salad

1 envelope LIPTON® RECIPE
    SECRETS® Vegetable Soup Mix
1 cup HELLMANN'S® or BEST
    FOODS® Real Mayonnaise
2 teaspoons white vinegar
2 pounds red or all-purpose
    potatoes, cooked and cut
    into chunks
¼ cup finely chopped red onion
    (optional)

1 package (6.9 ounces)
    RICE-A-RONI® With
    ⅓ Less Salt Chicken Flavor
3 tablespoons vegetable oil
2 cups chopped cooked chicken
    or turkey
1½ cups chopped tomato
1 cup frozen corn or 1 can
    (8 ounces) whole kernel corn,
    drained
½ cup chopped red or green bell
    pepper
¼ cup sliced green onions
2 to 3 tablespoons chopped cilantro
    or parsley
⅔ cup salsa or picante sauce
2 tablespoons lime or lemon juice

Vegetable Potato Salad

Prep Time: 20 minutes   Chill Time: 2 hours

Makes 6 servings

1. In large bowl, combine soup mix, mayonnaise and vinegar.

2. Add potatoes and onion; toss well. Chill 2 hours.

Santa Fe Rice Salad

Makes 5 servings

1. Prepare Rice-A-Roni® Mix as package directs, substituting 1 tablespoon oil for margarine. Cool 10 minutes.

2. In large bowl, combine prepared Rice-A-Roni®, chicken, tomato, corn, red pepper, onions and cilantro.

3. Combine salsa, lime juice and remaining 2 tablespoons oil. Pour over rice mixture; toss to coat. Cover; chill 4 hours or overnight. Stir before serving.

Vegetable Potato Salad

Mediterranean Orzo Salad

SALAD

1 cup orzo pasta
1 cup diced red bell pepper
½ cup crumbled feta cheese
1 can (2¼ ounces) sliced ripe olives, rinsed and drained
¼ cup chopped fresh basil *or* ½ teaspoon dried basil
Fresh basil leaves or parsley sprigs, for garnish (optional)

SALAD DRESSING

1 packet (1 ounce) HIDDEN VALLEY® The Original Ranch® Salad Dressing & Seasoning Mix
3 tablespoons olive oil
3 tablespoons red wine vinegar
1 teaspoon sugar

Makes 4 to 6 servings

Cook orzo according to package directions, omitting salt. Rinse with cold water and drain well. Combine orzo, bell pepper, cheese, olives and chopped fresh basil in a large bowl. (If using dried basil, add to dressing.) Whisk together salad dressing & seasoning mix, oil, vinegar and sugar. Stir dressing into orzo mixture. Cover and refrigerate at least 2 hours. Garnish with basil leaves before serving, if desired.

1 package (6 ounces) white and wild rice mix
1 *each* red and yellow bell pepper, seeded and chopped
¼ cup finely chopped red onion
¼ cup minced fresh parsley
¼ cup minced fresh basil leaves
⅓ cup **French's®** Honey Dijon Mustard
¼ cup olive oil
¼ cup red wine vinegar

Confetti Wild Rice Salad

Prep Time: 20 minutes   Cook Time: 20 minutes

Makes 8 side-dish servings

1. Prepare rice according to package directions; cool completely.

2. Place rice in large bowl. Add peppers, onion, parsley and basil. Combine mustard, oil and vinegar in small bowl; mix well. Pour over rice and vegetables; toss well to coat evenly. Cover and refrigerate 1 hour before serving. Garnish as desired.

Mediterranean Orzo Salad

Southwestern Chicken Taco Salad

Aluminum foil
Nonstick cooking spray
6 (8-inch) plain or flavored flour
   tortillas
2 (10-ounce) cans HORMEL® chunk
   breast of chicken, drained and
   flaked
1 tablespoon taco seasoning mix
2 tablespoons water
1 (15-ounce) can red kidney beans,
   drained and rinsed
1 (11-ounce) can whole kernel
   Mexican corn, drained
6 cups shredded lettuce
1 cup shredded Cheddar cheese
1 tomato, diced
1 avocado, diced
1 cup salsa, drained
½ cup sour cream

Makes 6 servings

Preheat oven to 350°F. Make six 2½-inch balls of foil by slightly crushing six 12×12-inch pieces of foil. Lightly spray one side of each flour tortilla and inside of six 10-ounce custard cups or small baking dishes with nonstick cooking spray. Gently press tortillas, sprayed sides up, into custard cups; folding edges to fit as necessary. Place ball of foil in each cup. Place cups on baking sheet. Bake tortilla shells 10 minutes; remove from oven and remove foil balls. Return to oven and continue baking an additional 3 to 5 minutes or until shells are crisp and edges are lightly browned.

Meanwhile, in skillet, combine chunk chicken, taco seasoning mix and water. Simmer over low heat 3 to 5 minutes. Add beans and corn. Heat until warmed through. Place 1 cup shredded lettuce into each tortilla shell. Fill with meat mixture. Top with cheese, tomato and avocado. In small bowl, combine salsa and sour cream. Drizzle dressing over salad.

quick tip

If you purchase an avocado that is not fully ripe, place it in a brown paper bag and keep it at room temperature. It will soften within a day or two. Avocados are ready to use when they yield to gentle pressure. Once ripe, avocados should be stored in the refrigerator, where they will last for five to seven days.

Southwestern Chicken Taco Salad

8 cups mixed fresh vegetables,
  such as broccoli, cauliflower,
  zucchini, carrots and red bell
  peppers, cut into 1- to 1½-inch
  pieces
⅓ cup distilled white vinegar
¼ cup sugar
¼ cup water
1 packet (1 ounce) HIDDEN VALLEY®
  The Original Ranch® Salad
  Dressing & Seasoning Mix

Sweet & Tangy Marinated Vegetables

Makes 8 servings

Place vegetables in a gallon-size Glad® Zipper Storage Bag. Combine vinegar, sugar, water and salad dressing & seasoning mix in a medium bowl. Whisk until sugar dissolves; pour over vegetables. Seal bag and shake to coat. Refrigerate 4 hours or overnight, turning bag occasionally.

Note: Vegetables will keep up to 3 days in refrigerator.

½ package (3 ounces) Oriental-flavor
  ramen noodle soup mix
1 (3-ounce) STARKIST Flavor Fresh
  Pouch® Tuna (Albacore or
  Chunk Light)
½ cup julienne-strip cucumber
½ cup julienne-strip green or red
  bell pepper
½ cup sliced water chestnuts, cut
  into halves

PEANUT DRESSING
2 tablespoons rice or white vinegar
2 teaspoons sesame oil
1 teaspoon peanut butter
⅛ teaspoon crushed red pepper

Tuna Ramen Noodle Salad

Prep Time: 15 minutes

Makes 1 serving

Cook ramen noodles according to package directions. Drain broth, reserving if desired to use as clear soup for another meal. In medium bowl toss noodles with tuna, cucumber, bell pepper and water chestnuts.

For Peanut Dressing, in small shaker jar combine vinegar, oil, peanut butter and crushed red pepper. Cover and shake until well blended. Toss with noodle mixture. Serve immediately.

Sweet & Tangy Marinated Vegetables

Refreshing Chicken & Rice Salad

1 package (4.3 ounces)
RICE-A-RONI® Long Grain
& Wild Rice Pilaf
1 tablespoon vegetable oil
2 cups chopped cooked chicken
2 carrots, sliced lengthwise, cut into
slices
1 cucumber, peeled, seeded, cut into
short thin strips
½ cup red or green bell pepper,
cut into short thin strips
2 tablespoons sliced green onions
⅓ cup Italian dressing
Lettuce

Makes 5 servings

1. Prepare Rice-A-Roni® Mix as package directs, substituting oil for margarine. Cool 10 minutes.

2. In large bowl, combine prepared Rice-A-Roni®, chicken, carrots, cucumber, bell pepper, onions and dressing. Chill 4 hours or overnight. Stir before serving.

3. Serve on lettuce-lined platter.

Original Ranch® Winter Vegetable Salad

1 packet (1 ounce) HIDDEN VALLEY®
The Original Ranch® Salad
Dressing & Seasoning Mix
½ cup cider vinegar
⅓ cup water
¼ cup olive oil
2 teaspoons sugar
7 cups assorted vegetable pieces*
such as broccoli, cauliflower
and carrots

Raw or cooked until crisp-tender.

Makes about 6 cups

Combine salad dressing & seasoning mix with vinegar, water, oil and sugar; set aside. Place vegetables in large resealable plastic bag or bowl. Pour dressing mixture over vegetables and shake well. Marinate in refrigerator 4 hours or overnight.

Refreshing Chicken & Rice Salad

Oriental Steak Salad

Prep Time: 10 minutes   Cook Time: 12 to 15 minutes

1 package (3 ounces) Oriental flavor
    instant ramen noodles,
    uncooked
4 cups water
1 bag (16 ounces) BIRDS EYE®
    frozen Cauliflower, Carrots
    & Snow Pea Pods
2 tablespoons vegetable oil
1 pound boneless beef top loin
    steak, cut into thin strips
⅓ cup Oriental sesame salad
    dressing
¼ cup chow mein noodles
    Lettuce leaves

Makes 4 servings

• Reserve seasoning packet from noodles.

• In large saucepan, bring water to boil. Add ramen noodles and vegetables; return to boil and cook 5 minutes, stirring occasionally. Drain.

• Heat oil in large nonstick skillet over medium-high heat. Add beef; cook and stir about 8 minutes or until browned.

• Stir in reserved seasoning packet until beef is well coated.

• In large bowl, toss together beef, vegetables, ramen noodles and salad dressing. Sprinkle with chow mein noodles. Serve over lettuce.

Serving Suggestion: This salad also can be served chilled. Moisten with additional salad dressing, if necessary. Sprinkle with chow mein noodles and spoon over lettuce just before serving.

Oriental Steak Salad

Beef in Wine Sauce (page 84)

quick-fix
casseroles & skillets

Quick Taco Macaroni & Cheese

Prep Time: 20 to 22 minutes   Cook Time: 30 to 35 minutes

1 package (12 ounces) large elbow
 macaroni (4 cups dried pasta)
1 tablespoon LAWRY'S® Seasoned
 Salt
1 pound lean ground beef or turkey
1 package (1 ounce) LAWRY'S® Taco
 Spices & Seasonings
2 cups (8 ounces) shredded Colby
 longhorn cheese
2 cups (8 ounces) shredded mild
 cheddar cheese
2 cups milk
3 eggs, beaten

Makes 6 to 8 servings

In large stockpot, boil macaroni in unsalted water just until tender. Drain and toss with Seasoned Salt. Meanwhile, in medium skillet, brown ground meat; drain fat. Stir in Taco Spices & Seasonings. Spray 13×9×2-inch baking dish with nonstick cooking spray. Layer half of macaroni in bottom of dish. Top with half of cheeses. Spread taco meat over top and repeat layers of macaroni and cheeses. In medium bowl, beat together milk and eggs. Pour egg mixture over top of casserole. Bake in preheated 350°F oven for 30 to 35 minutes or until golden brown.

Variation: For spicier flavor, try using LAWRY'S® Chili Spices & Seasonings OR Lawry's® Hot Taco Spices & Seasonings instead of Taco Spices & Seasonings.

Beef in Wine Sauce

4 pounds boneless beef chuck roast,
 cut into 1½- to 2-inch cubes
2 tablespoons garlic powder
2 cans (10¾ ounces each)
 condensed golden mushroom
 soup, undiluted
1 can (8 ounces) sliced mushrooms,
 drained
¾ cup dry sherry
1 envelope (about 1 ounce) dry
 onion soup mix
1 bag (20 ounces) frozen sliced
 carrots, thawed

Makes 6 to 8 servings

1. Preheat oven to 325°F. Spray heavy 4-quart casserole or Dutch oven with nonstick cooking spray.

2. Sprinkle beef with garlic powder. Place in prepared casserole.

3. Combine canned soup, mushrooms, sherry and dry soup mix in medium bowl. Pour over meat; mix well.

4. Cover; bake 3 hours or until meat is very tender. Add carrots during last 15 minutes of baking.

Quick Taco Macaroni & Cheese

Asian Noodles with Vegetables and Chicken

1 tablespoon vegetable oil
2 cups sliced shiitake mushrooms
    or button mushrooms
2 cups fresh snow peas, sliced
    diagonally in half
2 packages (1.6 ounces each)
    garlic and vegetable instant
    rice noodle soup mix
2 cups boiling water
2 packages (about 6 ounces each)
    refrigerated fully cooked
    chicken breast strips, cut
    into pieces
¼ teaspoon red pepper flakes
2 tablespoons fresh lime juice
1 tablespoon soy sauce
2 tablespoons chopped cilantro
    or sliced green onion

Makes 4 servings

1. Heat oil in large skillet over medium-high heat. Add mushrooms and snow peas; cook 2 to 3 minutes or until peas are crisp-tender. Remove from skillet; set aside.

2. Break up noodles in soup mix. Add noodles, one seasoning packet, water, chicken and red pepper flakes to skillet; mix well. Cook over medium-high heat 5 to 7 minutes or until liquid thickens. Stir in reserved vegetables, lime juice and soy sauce. Sprinkle with cilantro. Serve immediately.

Country Pork Skillet

4 boneless top loin pork chops,
    diced
1 (12-ounce) jar pork gravy
2 tablespoons ketchup
8 small red potatoes, diced
2 cups frozen mixed vegetables

Makes 4 servings

In large skillet, brown pork cubes. Stir in gravy, ketchup and potatoes; cover and simmer for 10 minutes. Stir in vegetables; cook for 10 to 15 minutes longer, until vegetables are tender.

*Favorite recipe from **National Pork Board***

Asian Noodles with Vegetables and Chicken

Fast 'n Easy Chili

1½ pounds ground beef
  1 envelope LIPTON® RECIPE
     SECRETS® Onion Soup Mix*
  1 can (15 to 19 ounces) red kidney
     or black beans, drained
1½ cups water
  1 can (8 ounces) tomato sauce
  4 teaspoons chili powder

Also terrific with LIPTON® RECIPE SECRETS® Onion Mushroom or Beefy Onion Soup Mix.

Makes 6 servings

1. In 12-inch skillet, brown ground beef over medium-high heat; drain.

2. Stir in remaining ingredients. Bring to a boil over high heat. Reduce heat to low and simmer covered, stirring occasionally, 20 minutes. Top hot chili with shredded Cheddar cheese, and serve over hot cooked rice, if desired.

First Alarm Chili: Add 5 teaspoons chili powder.

Second Alarm Chili: Add 2 tablespoons chili powder.

Third Alarm Chili: Add chili powder at your own risk.

Pork Chop & Wild Rice Bake

Prep Time: 5 minutes   Cook Time: 35 minutes

  1 package (6 ounces) seasoned
     long grain & wild rice mix
  2 cups water
1⅓ cups **French's®** French Fried
     Onions, divided
  1 package (10 ounces) frozen
     cut green beans, thawed
     and drained
¼ cup orange juice
  1 teaspoon grated orange peel
  4 boneless pork chops (1 inch thick)

Makes 4 servings

1. Preheat oven to 375°F. Combine rice mix and seasoning packet, water, ⅔ cup French Fried Onions, green beans, orange juice and orange peel in 2-quart shallow baking dish. Arrange pork chops on top.

2. Bake, uncovered, 30 minutes or until pork chops are no longer pink in center. Sprinkle chops with remaining ⅔ cup onions. Bake 5 minutes or until onions are golden.

Fast 'n Easy Chili

1 (2- to 2½-pound) whole chicken,
    cut into 8 pieces
2 teaspoons dried thyme
1 teaspoon paprika
1 teaspoon salt
½ teaspoon ground black pepper
2 tablespoons olive oil
8 large whole cloves garlic, peeled
¼ cup dry vermouth or water
2 tablespoons margarine or butter
1 (4.6-ounce) package PASTA
    RONI® Garlic & Olive Oil
    with Vermicelli
1½ cups fresh asparagus, cut into
    1½-inch pieces, or broccoli
    florets
1 cup sliced carrots

Bistro Chicken Skillet

Prep Time: 10 minutes   Cook Time: 30 minutes

Makes 4 servings

1. Sprinkle meaty side of chicken with thyme, paprika, salt and pepper. In large skillet over medium-high heat, heat oil. Add chicken, seasoned-side down. Cook 5 minutes. Reduce heat to medium-low; turn chicken over. Add garlic. Cover; cook 20 to 25 minutes or until chicken is no longer pink inside.

2. Meanwhile, in medium saucepan, bring 1½ cups water, vermouth and margarine just to a boil. Stir in pasta, asparagus, carrots and Special Seasonings. Reduce heat to medium. Gently boil uncovered, 10 minutes or until pasta is tender, stirring occasionally.

3. Remove chicken and garlic from skillet with slotted spoon. Skim off and discard fat from skillet juices. Serve chicken, garlic and reserved juices over pasta.

6 ounces uncooked ramen noodles
1 tablespoon olive oil
1 pound asparagus, cut into 1-inch
    pieces
1 red bell pepper, cut into thin rings
3 green onions, chopped
1 clove garlic, minced
1 pound sea scallops, halved
    crosswise
2 tablespoons soy sauce
1 teaspoon hot pepper sauce
1 teaspoon sesame oil
    Juice of ½ lime

Scallop Stir-Fry

Makes 4 servings

1. Cook noodles in lightly salted boiling water according to package directions.

2. Meanwhile, heat olive oil in large skillet or wok over high heat. Add asparagus, bell pepper, green onions and garlic; stir-fry 2 minutes. Add scallops; stir-fry until scallops turn opaque.

3. Stir in soy sauce, hot pepper sauce, sesame oil and lime juice. Add noodles; heat through, stirring occasionally.

Variation: Substitute vermicelli for ramen noodles.

Bistro Chicken Skillet

Biscuit and Sausage Bake

Prep Time: 10 minutes   Bake Time: 22 minutes

2 cups biscuit baking mix
½ cup milk
1 egg
1 teaspoon vanilla
1 cup fresh or frozen blueberries
6 fully cooked breakfast sausage
    links, thawed if frozen
Maple syrup, warmed

Makes 6 servings

1. Preheat oven to 350°F. Spray 8-inch square baking pan with nonstick cooking spray. Whisk baking mix, milk, egg and vanilla in medium bowl. Stir in blueberries. (Batter will be stiff.) Spread batter into prepared pan.

2. Cut each sausage link into small pieces; sprinkle pieces over batter. Bake 22 minutes or until lightly browned on top. Cut into squares; serve with maple syrup.

Garlic Shrimp with Wilted Spinach

2 teaspoons BERTOLLI® Olive Oil
1 pound uncooked medium shrimp,
    peeled and deveined
¼ cup diagonally sliced green onions
2 tablespoons sherry or dry white
    wine (optional)
1 envelope LIPTON® RECIPE
    SECRETS® Savory Herb
    with Garlic Soup Mix*
1½ cups water
1 large tomato, diced
2 cups fresh trimmed spinach leaves
    (about 4 ounces)
¼ cup chopped unsalted cashews
    (optional)

*Also terrific with LIPTON® RECIPE SECRETS® Golden Onion Soup Mix.

Makes about 4 servings

In 12-inch skillet, heat oil over medium heat and cook shrimp 2 minutes or until pink. Remove and set aside.

In same skillet, cook green onions, stirring occasionally, 2 minutes or until slightly soft. Add sherry and bring to a boil over high heat, stirring frequently. Stir in soup mix blended with water. Return to a boil over high heat. Reduce heat to low and simmer 5 minutes or until sauce is thickened. Stir in tomato and spinach. Simmer, covered, stirring once, 3 minutes or until spinach is cooked. Return shrimp to skillet and cook 1 minute or until heated through. Sprinkle with cashews.

Menu Suggestion: Serve with hot cooked rice and fresh fruit for dessert.

Biscuit and Sausage Bake

Empanada Pie

1 tablespoon vegetable oil
1 small onion, chopped
1 pound ground beef chuck
1 package (about 1 ounce) taco
    seasoning mix
1 can (8 ounces) tomato sauce
¼ cup raisins
2 teaspoons dark brown sugar
1 package (8 count) refrigerated
    crescent rolls
    Sliced green onion (optional)

Makes 4 to 6 servings

1. Preheat oven to 375°F. Grease 10-inch shallow round baking dish or deep-dish pie plate.

2. Heat oil in large skillet over medium-high heat. Add onion; cook 2 to 3 minutes or until translucent. Add ground beef; brown beef 6 to 8 minutes, stirring to break up meat. Drain fat. Sprinkle taco seasoning over beef mixture. Add tomato sauce, raisins and brown sugar. Reduce heat to low; cook 2 to 3 minutes.

3. Spoon beef mixture into prepared dish. Unroll crescent dough; divide into triangles. Arrange in spiral with points of dough towards center. Do not seal dough pieces together.

4. Bake 13 to 17 minutes or until dough is puffed and golden brown. Garnish with green onion, if desired.

Baked Penne & Ham

Prep Time: 15 minutes   Cook Time: 12 minutes

1 package (1.8 ounces) white
    sauce mix
2 cups milk
1½ cups (6 ounces) shredded fontina
    cheese, divided
3 cups cooked penne pasta (2 cups
    uncooked)
2 cups **French's**® French Fried
    Onions, divided
1 cup diced boiled ham
½ cup frozen peas
⅓ cup chopped oil-packed sun-dried
    tomatoes, drained

Makes 4 servings

1. Prepare white sauce mix according to package directions using 2 cups milk. Stir in 1 cup cheese. Cook over low heat, stirring constantly, until cheese melts.

2. Combine pasta, *1 cup* French Fried Onions, ham, peas and tomatoes in large bowl. Add cheese sauce and toss to coat. Transfer to shallow 2-quart microwave-safe dish.

3. Microwave, covered, on HIGH 5 minutes. Stir. Sprinkle with remaining *1 cup* onions and cheese. Microwave on HIGH 3 minutes or cheese is melted and onions are golden.

Empanada Pie

Chicken Florentine in Minutes

3 cups water
1 cup milk
2 tablespoons butter
2 packages (about 4 ounces each)
fettuccine Alfredo or stroganoff
pasta mix
4 cups fresh baby spinach, coarsely
chopped
¼ teaspoon black pepper
1 package (about 10 ounces)
refrigerated fully cooked
chicken breast strips, cut
into bite-size pieces
¼ cup diced roasted red peppers
¼ cup sour cream

Makes 4 servings

1. Bring water, milk and butter to a boil in large saucepan over medium-high heat. Stir in pasta mixes, spinach and black pepper. Reduce heat to medium; cook 8 minutes or until pasta is tender, stirring occasionally.

2. Stir in chicken and red peppers; cook 2 minutes or until hot. Remove from heat. Stir in sour cream.

Peppered Pork & Pilaf
Prep Time: 10 minutes   Total Time: 50 minutes

1 large size (20×14-inch) oven
cooking bag
2 tablespoons all-purpose flour
1 pound ALWAYS TENDER®
peppercorn flavored pork chops
2 medium green, red and/or yellow
bell peppers, cut into thin strips
1 red onion, cut into thin wedges
1 cup uncooked instant white rice
1 (1.2-ounce) package brown gravy
mix
2 teaspoons HERB-OX® reduced
sodium beef flavored bouillon
3 cups water

Makes 4 servings

Preheat oven to 350°F. Add flour to oven bag; twist end of bag and shake to coat with flour. Place oven bag into 13×9-inch baking dish. Add pork, bell peppers, onion, rice, gravy mix, bouillon and water. Gently squeeze bag to blend ingredients. Arrange ingredients in even layer in pan. Cut six (½-inch) slits in top of bag. Bake 40 minutes or until pork is cooked through.

Chicken Florentine in Minutes

2 tablespoons olive oil
1 cup uncooked white rice
1 can (about 14 ounces) diced
    tomatoes with garlic
1½ cups water
1 teaspoon Creole or Cajun
    seasoning blend
1 pound peeled cooked medium
    shrimp
1 package (10 ounces) frozen okra
    or 1½ cups frozen sugar snap
    peas, thawed

Creole Shrimp and Rice

Prep and Cook Time: 20 minutes

Makes 4 servings

1. Heat oil in large skillet over medium heat. Add rice; cook and stir 2 to 3 minutes or until lightly browned.

2. Add tomatoes, water and Creole seasoning; bring to a boil. Reduce heat; cover and simmer 15 minutes.

3. Add shrimp and okra; cover and cook 3 minutes or until heated through.

Note: Okra are oblong green pods. When cooked, okra gives off a viscous substance that acts as a good thickener.

4 large or 8 small chicken thighs
    (2 to 2½ pounds), trimmed
    of excess fat
2 teaspoons rotisserie or herb
    chicken seasoning*
1 tablespoon margarine or butter
3 cups (8 ounces) halved or
    quartered mushrooms
1 medium onion, coarsely chopped
½ cup dry white wine or vermouth
1 (4.9-ounce) package
    PASTA RONI® Homestyle
    Chicken Flavor
½ cup sliced green onions

* 1 teaspoon paprika and 1 teaspoon garlic salt can be substituted.

Coq au Vin & Pasta

Prep Time: 10 minutes   Cook Time: 30 minutes

Makes 4 servings

1. Sprinkle meaty side of chicken with rotisserie seasoning. In large skillet over medium-high heat, melt margarine. Add chicken, seasoned-side down; cook 3 minutes. Reduce heat to medium-low; turn chicken over.

2. Add mushrooms, onion and wine. Cover; simmer 15 to 18 minutes or until chicken is no longer pink inside. Remove chicken from skillet; set aside.

3. In same skillet, bring 1 cup water to a boil. Stir in pasta, green onions and Special Seasonings. Place chicken over pasta. Reduce heat to medium-low. Cover; gently boil 6 to 8 minutes or until pasta is tender. Let stand 3 to 5 minutes before serving.

Creole Shrimp and Rice

Broccoli, Turkey and Noodle Skillet

1 tablespoon butter
1 green bell pepper, chopped
1 cup frozen chopped broccoli, thawed
1/4 teaspoon black pepper
1 1/2 cups chicken broth
1/2 cup milk or half-and-half
2 cups diced cooked turkey breast
1 package (about 4 ounces) chicken and broccoli pasta mix
1/4 cup sour cream

Makes 4 servings

1. Melt butter in large nonstick skillet over medium-high heat. Add bell pepper, broccoli and black pepper; cook 5 minutes or until bell pepper is crisp-tender. Add chicken broth and milk; bring to a boil. Stir in turkey and pasta mix.

2. Reduce heat to low; cook 8 to 10 minutes or until noodles are tender. Remove from heat; stir in sour cream. Let stand, uncovered, 5 minutes or until sauce is thickened.

Thai-Style Beef & Rice

Prep Time: 15 minutes   Cook Time: 30 minutes

1 (6.2-ounce) package RICE-A-RONI® Fried Rice
2 tablespoons margarine or butter
1 pound boneless sirloin or top round steak, cut into thin strips
2 cloves garlic, minced
1/4 teaspoon crushed red pepper flakes
1 tablespoon sesame oil or vegetable oil
2 cups fresh or frozen snow peas, halved if large
1/2 cup red and/or yellow bell pepper strips
3 tablespoons soy sauce
1 tablespoon peanut butter
1/4 cup chopped cilantro (optional)

Makes 4 servings

1. In large skillet over medium heat, sauté rice-vermicelli mix with margarine until vermicelli is golden brown.

2. Slowly stir in 2 cups water and Special Seasonings; bring to a boil. Reduce heat to low. Cover; simmer 15 to 20 minutes or until rice is tender. Let stand 3 minutes.

3. Meanwhile, toss steak with garlic and red pepper flakes; set aside. In another large skillet or wok over medium-high heat, heat oil until hot. Add snow peas and bell pepper; stir-fry 2 minutes. Add beef mixture; stir-fry 2 minutes. Add soy sauce and peanut butter; stir-fry 1 minute or until beef is barely pink inside and vegetables are crisp-tender. Serve beef mixture over rice; sprinkle with cilantro, if desired.

Broccoli, Turkey and Noodle Skillet

Chicken, Asparagus & Mushroom Bake

1 tablespoon butter
1 tablespoon olive oil
2 boneless skinless chicken breasts (about ½ pound), cut into bite-size pieces
2 cloves garlic, minced
1 cup sliced mushrooms
2 cups sliced asparagus
Black pepper
1 package (about 6 ounces) corn bread stuffing mix
¼ cup dry white wine (optional)
1 can (about 14½ ounces) reduced-sodium chicken broth
1 can (about 10½ ounces) condensed condensed cream of asparagus or cream of chicken soup, undiluted

Makes 6 servings

1. Preheat oven to 350°F. Heat butter and oil in large skillet until butter is melted. Cook and stir chicken and garlic about 3 minutes over medium-high heat until chicken is no longer pink. Add mushrooms; cook and stir 2 minutes. Add asparagus; cook and stir about 5 minutes or until asparagus is crisp-tender. Season with pepper to taste.

2. Transfer mixture to 2½-quart casserole or 6 small casseroles. Top with stuffing mix.

3. Add wine to skillet, if desired; cook and stir 1 minute over medium-high heat, scraping up any browned bits from bottom of skillet. Add chicken broth and soup; cook and stir until well blended.

4. Pour broth mixture into casserole; mix well. Bake, uncovered, about 35 minutes (30 minutes for small casseroles) or until heated through and lightly browned.

Note: This recipe is a perfect way to stretch a little leftover chicken into an easy and tasty dinner.

Serving Suggestion: Serve with tossed green salad and sliced tomatoes.

Chicken, Asparagus & Mushroom Bake

Broccoli-Stuffed Shells

1 tablespoon butter or margarine
¼ cup chopped onion
1 cup ricotta cheese
1 egg
2 cups chopped cooked broccoli *or* 1 package (10 ounces) frozen chopped broccoli, thawed and well drained
1 cup (4 ounces) shredded Monterey Jack cheese
20 jumbo pasta shells
1 can (28 ounces) crushed tomatoes in purée
1 packet (1 ounce) HIDDEN VALLEY® The Original Ranch® Salad Dressing & Seasoning Mix
¼ cup grated Parmesan cheese

Makes 4 servings

Preheat oven to 350°F. In a small skillet, melt butter over medium heat. Add onion; cook until onion is tender but not browned. Remove from heat; cool. In a large bowl, stir ricotta cheese and egg until well blended. Add broccoli and Monterey Jack cheese; mix well. In a large pot of boiling water, cook pasta shells 8 to 10 minutes or just until tender; drain. Rinse under cold running water; drain again. Stuff each shell with about 2 tablespoons broccoli-cheese mixture.

In a medium bowl, combine tomatoes, sautéed onion and salad dressing & seasoning mix; mix well. Pour one third of the tomato mixture into a 13×9-inch baking dish. Arrange filled shells in dish. Spoon remaining tomato mixture over top. Sprinkle with Parmesan cheese. Bake, covered, until hot and bubbly, about 30 minutes.

Jamaican Pork Skillet

Prep and Cook Time: 20 minutes

1 tablespoon vegetable oil
4 well-trimmed center cut pork chops, cut ½ inch thick
¾ teaspoon blackened or Cajun seasoning blend
¼ teaspoon ground allspice
1 cup chunky salsa, divided
1 can (15 ounces) black beans, rinsed and drained
1 can (about 8 ounces) whole kernel corn, drained or 1 cup thawed frozen whole kernel corn
1 tablespoon fresh lime juice

Makes 4 servings

1. Heat oil in large deep skillet over medium-high heat. Sprinkle both sides of pork chops with blackened seasoning and allspice; cook 2 minutes per side or until browned.

2. Pour ½ cup salsa over pork chops; reduce heat to medium. Cover and simmer about 12 minutes or until pork is no longer pink.

3. While pork chops are simmering, combine beans, corn, remaining ½ cup salsa and lime juice in medium bowl; mix well. Serve bean mixture with pork chops.

Tip: For extra flavor, add chopped fresh cilantro to the bean mixture.

Broccoli-Stuffed Shells

30-Minute Paella

2 tablespoons olive oil
1 package (about 10 ounces) chicken-flavored rice and vermicelli mix
¼ teaspoon red pepper flakes
3½ cups water
1 package (about 10 ounces) refrigerated fully cooked chicken breast strips, cut into pieces
1 package (8 ounces) medium raw shrimp, peeled
1 cup frozen peas
¼ cup diced roasted red pepper

Makes 6 servings

1. Heat oil in large skillet over medium heat. Add rice mix and red pepper flakes; cook and stir 2 minutes or until vermicelli is golden.

2. Add water, chicken, shrimp, peas and roasted red pepper. Bring to a boil. Reduce heat to low. Cover and cook 12 to 15 minutes or until rice is tender, stirring occasionally.

Mexican Turkey Chili Mac

1 pound ground turkey
1 package (1¼ ounces) reduced-sodium taco seasoning mix
1 can (14½ ounces) reduced-sodium stewed tomatoes
1 can (11 ounces) corn with red and green peppers, undrained
1½ cups cooked elbow macaroni, without salt, drained
1 ounce low-salt corn chips, crushed
½ cup shredded reduced-fat Cheddar cheese

Makes 6 servings

1. In large nonstick skillet, over medium-high heat, sauté turkey 5 to 6 minutes or until no longer pink; drain. Stir in taco seasoning, tomatoes, corn and macaroni. Reduce heat to medium and cook 4 to 5 minutes until heated through.

2. Sprinkle corn chips over meat mixture and top with cheese. Cover and heat 1 to 2 minutes or until cheese is melted.

*Favorite recipe from **National Turkey Federation***

30-Minute Paella

Spicy Chicken Casserole with Cornbread

2 tablespoons olive oil
4 boneless skinless chicken breasts, cut into bite-size pieces
1 package (about 1 ounce) taco seasoning mix
1 can (about 15 ounces) black beans, rinsed and drained
1 can (14½ ounces) diced tomatoes, drained
1 can (about 10 ounces) Mexican-style corn, drained
1 can (about 4 ounces) diced mild green chiles, drained
½ cup mild salsa
1 box (about 8½ ounces) corn bread mix, plus ingredients to prepare mix
½ cup (2 ounces) shredded Cheddar cheese
¼ cup chopped red bell pepper

Makes 4 to 6 servings

1. Preheat oven to 350°F. Spray 2-quart casserole with nonstick cooking spray. Set aside. Heat oil in large skillet over medium heat. Cook chicken until no longer pink in center.

2. Sprinkle taco seasoning over chicken. Add black beans, tomatoes, corn, chiles and salsa; stir until well blended. Transfer to prepared dish.

3. Prepare cornbread mix according to package directions, adding cheese and bell pepper. Spread batter over chicken mixture.

4. Bake 30 minutes or until cornbread is golden brown.

quick tip

Casserole dishes are measured by their volume in quarts. If you are not sure of the size of your dish, it can be measured by filling the dish full with water and then measuring the water. The most common sizes of casseroles are 1, 1½, 2, 2½ and 3 quarts.

Spicy Chicken Casserole with Cornbread

Easy Asian Chicken Skillet

Prep Time: 5 minutes   Cook Time: 20 minutes

2 packages (3 ounces each) chicken-flavored instant ramen noodles
1 package (10 ounces) frozen broccoli florets, thawed
1 package (9 ounces) frozen baby carrots, thawed
1 tablespoon vegetable oil
1 pound boneless skinless chicken breasts, cut into thin strips
1 can (8 ounces) sliced water chestnuts, drained
¼ cup stir-fry sauce

Makes 4 to 6 servings

1. Remove seasoning packets from noodles. Save one packet for another use.

2. Bring 4 cups water to a boil in large saucepan. Add noodles, broccoli and carrots. Cook over medium-high heat 5 minutes, stirring occasionally; drain.

3. Heat oil in large nonstick skillet over medium-high heat. Add chicken; cook and stir about 8 minutes or until browned.

4. Stir in noodle mixture, water chestnuts, stir-fry sauce and one seasoning packet; cook until heated through.

Skillet Beef & Broccoli

Prep Time: 10 minutes   Cook Time: 15 minutes

1 tablespoon BERTOLLI® Olive Oil
1 pound sirloin steak, cut into 1-inch strips
1 package (10 ounces) frozen broccoli florets, thawed
1 envelope LIPTON® RECIPE SECRETS® Onion Soup Mix*
1¼ cups water
1 tablespoon firmly packed brown sugar
1 tablespoon soy sauce

Makes 4 servings

1. In 12-inch nonstick skillet, heat oil over medium-high heat; brown steak, stirring occasionally, in two batches. Remove steak from skillet and set aside.

2. Stir in broccoli, soup mix blended with water, brown sugar and soy sauce. Bring to a boil over high heat. Reduce heat to low and simmer uncovered, stirring occasionally, 2 minutes.

3. Return steak to skillet and cook 1 minute or until steak is done. Serve, if desired, with hot cooked rice.

*Also terrific with LIPTON® RECIPE SECRETS® Onion Mushroom Soup Mix.

Easy Asian Chicken Skillet

Saffron Chicken & Vegetables

2 tablespoons vegetable oil

6 bone-in chicken thighs, skinned

1 bag (16 ounces) frozen mixed vegetables, such as broccoli, red bell peppers, mushrooms and onions, thawed

1 can (about 14 ounces) roasted garlic-flavored chicken broth

1 can (10¾ ounces) condensed cream of chicken soup, undiluted

1 can (10¾ ounces) condensed cream of mushroom soup, undiluted

1 package (about 8 ounces) uncooked saffron yellow rice mix with seasonings

½ cup water

1 teaspoon paprika (optional)

Makes 6 servings

1. Preheat oven to 350°F. Spray 3-quart casserole with nonstick cooking spray; set aside.

2. Heat oil in large skillet over medium heat. Brown chicken on both sides; drain fat.

3. Meanwhile, combine vegetables, chicken broth, soups, rice mix with seasonings and water in large bowl; mix well. Place mixture in prepared casserole. Top with chicken. Sprinkle with paprika, if desired. Cover; bake 1½ hours or until chicken is no longer pink in center.

quick tip

When testing bone-in chicken pieces for doneness, you should be able to insert a fork into the chicken with ease and the juices should run clear. However, the meat and juices nearest the bones might still be a little pink even though the chicken is cooked through.

Saffron Chicken & Vegetables

1 pound zucchini, halved and cut
    into ½-inch slices (about 4 cups)
1 red or green bell pepper, cut into
    1-inch pieces
1 rib celery, thinly sliced
1 clove garlic, minced
2 cans (15 to 19 ounces each)
    kidney beans, rinsed and
    drained
1 can (28 ounces) crushed tomatoes
    in purée, undrained
¼ cup **Frank's® RedHot®** Original
    Cayenne Pepper Sauce
1 tablespoon chili powder
1 package (6½ ounces) cornbread
    mix, plus ingredients to prepare
    mix

Vegetarian Chili with Cornbread Topping

Prep Time: 20 minutes   Cook Time: 35 minutes

Makes 6 servings

1. Preheat oven to 400°F. Heat *1 tablespoon oil* in 12-inch heatproof skillet* over medium-high heat. Add zucchini, bell pepper, celery and garlic. Cook and stir 5 minutes or until tender. Stir in beans, tomatoes, **Frank's RedHot** Sauce and chili powder. Heat to boiling, stirring.

2. Prepare cornbread mix according to package directions. Spoon batter on top of chili mixture, spreading to ½ inch from edges. Bake 30 minutes or until cornbread is golden brown and mixture is bubbly.

If handle of skillet is not heatproof, wrap in foil.

2 cups cooked chicken, cut in strips
8 ounces penne or other pasta,
    cooked and drained
1 pound cooked vegetables, cut in
    wedges (about 5 cups)
1 packet (1 ounce) HIDDEN VALLEY®
    The Original Ranch® Salad
    Dressing & Seasoning Mix
¾ cup chicken broth
¼ cup grated Parmesan cheese

Primavera Light

Makes 4 to 6 servings

In a skillet, combine chicken, pasta and vegetables. Stir salad dressing & seasoning mix into chicken broth; pour into skillet. Cook and stir over low heat until hot. Stir in cheese; serve immediately.

Vegetarian Chili with Cornbread Topping

Bayou-Style Pot Pie

Prep and Cook Time: 28 minutes

1 tablespoon olive oil
1 large onion, chopped
1 green bell pepper, chopped
1½ teaspoons minced garlic
½ pound boneless skinless chicken
    thighs, cut into 1-inch pieces
1 can (14½ ounces) stewed tomatoes
½ pound fully cooked smoked sausage
    or kielbasa, thinly sliced
¾ to 1½ teaspoons hot pepper sauce
2¼ cups buttermilk baking mix
¾ teaspoon dried thyme
⅛ teaspoon black pepper
⅔ cup milk

Makes 4 servings

1. Preheat oven to 450°F. Heat oil in medium ovenproof skillet over medium-high heat until hot. Add onion, bell pepper and garlic; cook 3 minutes, stirring occasionally.

2. Add chicken; cook 1 minute. Add tomatoes, sausage and hot sauce; cook over medium-low heat 5 minutes.

3. Meanwhile, combine baking mix, thyme and black pepper. Stir in milk. Drop batter by heaping tablespoonfuls in mounds over chicken mixture. Bake 14 minutes or until biscuits are golden brown and cooked through and chicken mixture is bubbly.

Tip: Andouille, a spicy Louisiana-style sausage, is perfect for this dish.

Tuna and Rice Skillet Dinner

Prep Time: 30 minutes

1 package (6½ ounces) chicken
    flavored rice mix
½ cup chopped onion
1½ cups frozen peas and carrots,
    thawed
1 can (10¾ ounces) cream of
    mushroom soup
⅛ teaspoon ground black pepper
1 (7-ounce) STARKIST Flavor Fresh
    Pouch® Tuna (Albacore or
    Chunk Light)
⅓ cup toasted slivered almonds
    (optional)

Makes 4 to 6 servings

In medium saucepan, combine rice mix and onion; add water according to package directions. Prepare rice according to package directions. Stir in vegetables, soup and pepper; blend well. Simmer, covered, 5 to 7 minutes, stirring occasionally. Stir in tuna; serve with almonds, if desired.

Bayou-Style Pot Pie

Indian-Spiced Chicken with Wild Rice

½ teaspoon salt
½ teaspoon ground cumin
½ teaspoon black pepper
¼ teaspoon ground cinnamon
¼ teaspoon ground turmeric
4 boneless skinless chicken breasts
    (about 1 pound)
2 tablespoons olive oil
2 carrots, sliced
1 red bell pepper, chopped
1 stalk celery, chopped
2 cloves garlic, minced
1 package (6 ounces) long grain
    and wild rice mix
2 cups reduced-sodium chicken
    broth
1 cup raisins
¼ cup sliced almonds

Makes 4 servings

1. Combine salt, cumin, black pepper, cinnamon and turmeric in small bowl. Rub spice mixture on both sides of chicken. Place chicken on plate; cover and refrigerate 30 minutes.

2. Preheat oven to 350°F. Spray 13×9-inch baking dish with nonstick cooking spray.

3. Heat oil in large skillet over medium-high heat. Add chicken; cook 2 minutes per side or until browned. Remove chicken; set aside.

4. Add carrots, bell pepper, celery and garlic to same skillet; cook and stir 2 minutes. Add rice; cook 5 minutes, stirring frequently. Add seasoning packet from rice mix and chicken broth; bring to a boil over high heat. Remove from heat; stir in raisins. Pour into prepared dish. Place chicken on rice mixture; sprinkle with almonds.

5. Cover tightly with foil and bake 35 minutes or until chicken is no longer pink in center and rice is tender.

Indian-Spiced Chicken with Wild Rice

Super Chili for a Crowd (*page 122*)

no-fuss family
favorites

Spiced Turkey with Fruit Salsa

1 turkey breast tenderloin (6 ounces)
2 teaspoons lime juice
1 teaspoon mesquite seasoning
  blend or ground cumin
½ cup frozen pitted sweet cherries,
  thawed and cut into halves*
¼ cup chunky salsa

Drained canned sweet cherries can be substituted for frozen cherries.

Makes 2 servings

1. Prepare grill for direct grilling. Brush both sides of turkey with lime juice. Sprinkle with mesquite seasoning.

2. Grill turkey over medium heat 15 to 20 minutes or until turkey is no longer pink in center and juices run clear, turning once.

3. Meanwhile, stir together cherries and salsa.

4. Thinly slice turkey. To serve, spoon salsa mixture over turkey.

Super Chili for a Crowd
Prep Time: 15 minutes   Cook Time: 1 hour 15 minutes

2 large onions, chopped
1 tablespoon minced garlic
2 pounds boneless top round or
  sirloin steak, cut into ½-inch
  cubes
1 pound ground beef
1 can (28 ounces) crushed tomatoes
  in purée
1 can (15 to 19 ounces) red kidney
  beans, undrained
⅓ cup **Frank's® RedHot®** Original
  Cayenne Pepper Sauce
2 packages (1¼ ounces each) chili
  seasoning mix

Makes 10 servings

1. Heat *1 tablespoon oil* in 5-quart saucepot or Dutch oven until hot. Sauté onion and garlic until tender; transfer to bowl.

2. Heat *3 tablespoons oil* in same pot; cook meat in batches until well browned. Drain fat.

3. Add *¾ cup water* and remaining ingredients to pot. Stir in onion and garlic. Heat to boiling, stirring. Simmer, partially covered, for 1 hour or until meat is tender, stirring often. Garnish as desired.

Spiced Turkey with Fruit Salsa

Zesty Steak Fajitas

Prep Time: 5 minutes   Cook Time: 15 minutes

¾ cup **French's®** Worcestershire
    Sauce, divided
1 pound boneless top round, sirloin
    or flank steak
3 tablespoons taco seasoning mix
2 red or green bell peppers, cut into
    quarters
1 to 2 large onions, cut into thick
    slices
¾ cup chili sauce
8 (8-inch) flour or corn tortillas,
    heated
    Sour cream and shredded cheese
    (optional)

Makes 4 servings

1. Pour ½ cup Worcestershire over steak in deep dish. Cover and refrigerate 30 minutes or up to 3 hours. Drain meat and rub both sides with seasoning mix. Discard marinade.

2. Grill meat and vegetables over medium-hot coals 10 to 15 minutes or until meat is medium-rare and vegetables are charred but tender.

3. Thinly slice meat and vegetables. Place in large bowl. Add chili sauce and remaining ¼ cup Worcestershire. Toss to coat. Serve in tortillas and garnish with sour cream and cheese.

Saucepot Spinach Lasagne

Prep Time: 20 minutes

1 package KNORR® Recipe
    Classics™ Leek recipe mix
3 cups water
8 ounces uncooked wide egg
    noodles (about 6 cups)
1 cup milk
1 package (10 ounces) frozen leaf
    spinach, thawed
2 cups shredded mozzarella cheese,
    divided (about 8 ounces)
⅓ cup grated Parmesan cheese

Makes 4 servings

• In 4-quart saucepot, combine recipe mix and water. Add noodles and milk. Heat to boiling, stirring frequently. Reduce heat; simmer 5 minutes, stirring occasionally.

• Add spinach; heat to simmering. Stir in 1 cup mozzarella and Parmesan cheese. Spoon into shallow serving bowl and sprinkle with remaining mozzarella cheese.

Zesty Steak Fajitas

Curried Shrimp and Noodles

3 cups water
2 packages (about 1.6 ounces each) instant curry-flavored rice noodle soup mix
1 package (8 ounces) frozen cooked baby shrimp
1 cup frozen bell pepper strips, cut into 1-inch pieces, or frozen peas
¼ cup chopped green onions
¼ teaspoon salt
¼ teaspoon black pepper
1 to 2 tablespoons fresh lime juice

Makes 4 servings

1. Bring 3 cups water to a boil in large saucepan over high heat. Add soup mix, shrimp, bell pepper, green onions, salt and black pepper.

2. Cook 3 to 5 minutes, stirring frequently, or until noodles are tender. Stir in lime juice. Serve immediately.

Mustard Crusted Chicken & Rice

Prep Time: 5 minutes   Cook Time: 35 minutes

1 (6.5-ounce) package RICE-A-RONI® Broccoli Au Gratin
2½ tablespoons margarine or butter
1½ cups baby carrots, cut crosswise into halves
½ cup sliced green onions
¼ cup brown mustard
1 tablespoon honey
2 cloves garlic, minced
4 bone-in, skin-on chicken breasts (1 to 1½ pounds)

Makes 4 servings

1. Preheat broiler. In large skillet over medium heat, sauté rice-vermicelli mix with margarine until vermicelli is light golden brown. Slowly stir in 2¼ cups water, carrots and Special Seasonings; bring to a boil. Reduce heat to low. Cover; simmer 15 to 20 minutes or until rice is tender. Stir in green onions; let stand 5 minutes.

2. Meanwhile, combine mustard, honey and garlic. Place chicken, meaty-side down, on broiler pan. Broil chicken 10 minutes. Turn chicken over and brush with half of mustard mixture. Broil 10 to 15 minutes or until chicken is no longer pink inside, brushing chicken once more with remaining mustard mixture. Serve chicken over rice.

Curried Shrimp and Noodles

1 envelope LIPTON® RECIPE
    SECRETS® Onion Soup Mix*
½ cup water
1½ pounds ground beef
½ cup shredded Swiss cheese
    (about 2 ounces)
1 tablespoon crisp-cooked crumbled
    bacon or bacon bits
½ teaspoon caraway seeds (optional)

*Also terrific with LIPTON® RECIPE
SECRETS® Onion Mushroom Soup Mix.

2 packages (3 ounces each) Oriental
    flavor instant ramen noodles
2 cups BIRDS EYE® frozen Broccoli,
    Carrots and Water Chestnuts
⅓ cup hot water
¼ cup creamy peanut butter
1 teaspoon sugar
⅛ to ¼ teaspoon crushed red pepper
    flakes

Grilled Reuben Burger

Makes 6 servings

1. In large bowl, combine all ingredients; shape into 6 patties.

2. Grill or broil until done. Top, if desired, with heated sauerkraut and additional bacon.

Thai Noodles with Peanut Sauce

Prep Time: 5 minutes   Cook Time: 10 minutes

Makes about 4 servings

• Reserve seasoning packets from noodles.

• Bring 4 cups water to boil in large saucepan. Add noodles and vegetables. Cook 3 minutes, stirring occasionally; drain.

• Meanwhile, whisk together hot water, peanut butter, sugar, red pepper flakes and reserved seasoning packets in large bowl until blended.

• Add noodles and vegetables; toss to coat. Serve warm.

Serving Suggestion: Add shredded carrot, thinly sliced cucumber or green onion for additional flavor and color. For a heartier main dish, add cooked seafood, shredded cooked chicken or pork.

Grilled Reuben Burger

Easy Cheese & Tomato Macaroni

Prep Time: 5 minutes   Cook Time: 15 minutes

2 packages (7 ounces each)
    macaroni and cheese dinner
1 tablespoon olive or vegetable oil
1 cup finely chopped onion
1 cup thinly sliced celery
1 can (28 ounces) CONTADINA®
    Recipe Ready Crushed
    Tomatoes
  Grated Parmesan cheese (optional)
  Sliced green onion or celery leaves
    (optional)

Makes 6 to 8 servings

1. Cook macaroni (from macaroni and cheese dinner) according to package directions; drain.

2. Heat oil in large skillet. Add chopped onion and celery; sauté for 3 minutes or until vegetables are tender.

3. Combine tomatoes and cheese mixes from dinners in small bowl. Stir into vegetable mixture.

4. Simmer for 3 to 4 minutes or until mixture is thickened and heated through. Add macaroni to skillet; stir until well coated with sauce. Heat thoroughly, stirring occasionally. Sprinkle with Parmesan cheese and sliced green onion, if desired.

Shrimp Alfredo with Sugar Snap Peas

Prep Time: 5 minutes   Cook Time: 15 minutes

½ cup milk
3 tablespoons margarine or butter
1 (4.7-ounce) package PASTA
    RONI® Fettuccine Alfredo
1 (9-ounce) package frozen sugar
    snap peas, thawed
8 ounces cooked deveined peeled
    medium shrimp
½ teaspoon ground lemon pepper

Makes 4 servings

1. In large saucepan, bring 1¼ cups water, milk, margarine, pasta and Special Seasonings to a boil. Reduce heat to low. Gently boil 4 minutes, stirring occasionally.

2. Stir in snap peas, shrimp and lemon pepper; cook 1 to 2 minutes or until pasta is tender. Let stand 3 minutes before serving.

Tip: If you don't have lemon pepper in your cupboard, try Italian seasoning instead.

Easy Cheese & Tomato Macaroni

Harvest Pot Roast with Sweet Potatoes

1 envelope LIPTON® RECIPE
    SECRETS® Onion Soup Mix
1½ cups water
¼ cup soy sauce
2 tablespoons firmly packed dark
    brown sugar
1 teaspoon ground ginger (optional)
1 (3- to 3½-pound) boneless pot
    roast (rump, chuck or round)
4 large sweet potatoes, peeled,
    if desired, and cut into large
    chunks
3 tablespoons water
2 tablespoons all-purpose flour

Makes 6 servings

1. Preheat oven to 325°F. In Dutch oven or 5-quart heavy ovenproof saucepan, combine soup mix, water, soy sauce, brown sugar and ginger; add roast.

2. Cover and bake 1 hour 45 minutes.

3. Add potatoes and bake covered an additional 45 minutes or until beef and potatoes are tender.

4. Remove roast and potatoes to serving platter and keep warm; reserve juices.

5. In small cup, with wire whisk, blend water and flour. In same Dutch oven, add flour mixture to reserved juices. Bring to a boil over high heat. Boil, stirring occasionally, 2 minutes. Serve with roast and potatoes.

Heinz® "TK" Tacoz

1 pound ground turkey or beef
1 package (1¼ ounces) taco
    seasoning mix
½ cup water
½ cup HEINZ® Tomato Ketchup
10 taco shells
    Shredded lettuce
    Chopped tomatoes
    Shredded Cheddar cheese
    Sour cream

Makes 5 servings (2 tacos each)

In large nonstick skillet over medium heat, cook turkey until no longer pink. Stir in taco seasoning and water. Simmer 2 minutes or until slightly thickened. Stir in ketchup; heat. Spoon mixture into taco shells. Top with lettuce, tomatoes, cheese and sour cream as desired.

Harvest Pot Roast with Sweet Potatoes

Tex-Mex Chicken & Rice Chili

1 package (6.8 ounces)
    RICE-A-RONI® Spanish Rice
2 cups chopped cooked chicken or
    turkey
1 can (15 or 16 ounces) kidney
    beans or pinto beans, rinsed
    and drained
1 can (14½ ounces) tomatoes or
    stewed tomatoes, undrained
1 medium green bell pepper, cut
    into ½-inch pieces
1½ teaspoons chili powder
1 teaspoon ground cumin
½ cup (2 ounces) shredded Cheddar
    or Monterey Jack cheese
    (optional)
Sour cream (optional)
Chopped cilantro (optional)

Makes 4 servings

1. In 3-quart saucepan, combine rice-vermicelli mix, Special Seasonings, 2¾ cups water, chicken, beans, tomatoes, green pepper, chili powder and cumin. Bring to a boil over high heat.

2. Reduce heat to low; simmer, uncovered, about 20 minutes or until rice is tender, stirring occasionally.

3. Top with cheese, sour cream and cilantro, if desired.

quick tip

When a recipe calls for chopped cooked chicken, it can be difficult to judge how much chicken to purchase. As a guideline, two whole chicken breasts (about 10 ounces each) will yield about 2 cups of chopped cooked chicken; one broiling/frying chicken (about 3 pounds) will yield about 2½ cups chopped cooked chicken. Leftover chicken and supermarket rotisserie chicken are also perfect for use in recipes like this one.

Tex-Mex Chicken & Rice Chili

Sonoma® Pot Pie

2 cans (10½ ounces each) chicken
   gravy
3 cups cooked chicken or turkey
   chunks
1 package (10 ounces) frozen mixed
   vegetables
⅔ cup SONOMA® Dried Tomato Bits
1 can (3 ounces drained weight)
   sliced mushrooms
¼ cup water
1½ teaspoons dried thyme leaves,
   divided
2¼ cups reduced-fat buttermilk
   baking mix
¾ cup plus 2 tablespoons lowfat milk

Makes 4 to 6 servings

Preheat oven to 450°F. In 3-quart saucepan, combine gravy, chicken, vegetables, tomato bits, mushrooms, water and ½ teaspoon thyme. Stir occasionally over medium-low heat until mixture comes to a boil. Meanwhile, in large bowl, combine baking mix, milk and remaining 1 teaspoon thyme; mix just to blend thoroughly. Pour chicken mixture into shallow 2-quart casserole or 9-inch square baking dish. Top with large spoonfuls of dough, making equal-sized mounds. Place casserole on baking sheet and bake about 20 minutes or until chicken mixture is bubbly and topping is golden brown.

Cranberry-Onion Pork Roast

1 boneless pork loin roast
   (about 2 pounds)
1 can (16 ounces) whole berry
   cranberry sauce
1 package (1 ounce) dry onion
   soup mix

Makes 4 to 6 servings

Season roast with salt and black pepper; place over indirect heat on grill. Stir together cranberry sauce and onion soup mix in small microwavable bowl. Heat, covered, in microwave until hot, about 1 minute. Baste roast with cranberry mixture every 10 minutes until roast is done (internal temperature registers 155° to 160°F on meat thermometer), about 30 to 45 minutes. Let roast rest about 5 to 8 minutes before slicing to serve. Heat any leftover basting mixture to boiling; stir and boil for 5 minutes. Serve alongside roast.

*Favorite recipe from **National Pork Board***

Sonoma® Pot Pie

Hearty BBQ Beef Sandwiches

1 envelope LIPTON® RECIPE
   SECRETS® Onion Soup Mix
2 cups water
½ cup chili sauce
¼ cup firmly packed light brown
   sugar
1 (3-pound) boneless chuck roast
8 kaiser rolls or hamburger buns,
   toasted

Makes 8 servings

1. Preheat oven to 325°F. In Dutch oven or 5-quart heavy ovenproof saucepan, combine soup mix, water, chili sauce and sugar; add roast.

2. Cover and bake 3 hours or until roast is tender.

3. Remove roast; reserve juices. Bring reserved juices to a boil over high heat. Boil 4 minutes.

4. Meanwhile, with fork, shred roast. Stir roast into reserved juices and simmer, stirring frequently, 1 minute. Serve on rolls.

Tip: Always measure brown sugar in a dry measure cup and pack down firmly. To soften hardened brown sugar, place in glass dish with 1 slice of bread. Cover with plastic wrap and microwave at HIGH 30 to 40 seconds. Let stand 30 seconds; stir. Remove bread.

Spinach & Feta Burgers

Prep Time: 10 minutes   Cook Time: 12 minutes

1 package KNORR® Recipe
   Classics™ Cream of Spinach
   recipe mix
2 pounds ground beef
½ cup water
4 ounces feta cheese, crumbled
1 tablespoon finely chopped garlic

Makes 8 servings

In large bowl, combine all ingredients; shape into 8 patties. Grill or broil until done. Serve, if desired, on rolls with lettuce and tomato.

Hearty BBQ Beef Sandwich

Refried Bean Tostadas

1 can (16 ounces) ORTEGA®
Refried Beans
¼ cup chopped onion
1 package (1¼ ounces) ORTEGA
Taco Seasoning Mix
1 package (10) ORTEGA Tostada
Shells, warmed
2 cups shredded lettuce
½ cup (2 ounces) shredded cheddar
cheese
⅓ cup sliced ripe olives
2 medium ripe avocados, cut into
20 slices
¾ cup ORTEGA Thick & Smooth
Taco Sauce

Makes 10 servings

COMBINE beans, onion and seasoning mix in medium saucepan. Cook, stirring frequently, for 4 to 5 minutes or until heated through.

SPREAD *¼ cup* bean mixture over each shell. Top with lettuce, cheese, olives, avocado and taco sauce.

The Original Ranch® Crispy Chicken

¼ cup unseasoned bread crumbs or
corn flake crumbs
1 packet (1 ounce) HIDDEN VALLEY®
The Original Ranch® Salad
Dressing & Seasoning Mix
6 bone-in chicken pieces

Makes 4 to 6 servings

Combine bread crumbs and salad dressing & seasoning mix in a resealable plastic bag. Add chicken pieces; seal bag. Shake to coat chicken. Bake chicken on an ungreased baking sheet at 375°F 50 minutes or until no longer pink in center and juices run clear.

Refried Bean Tostada

Cheddar Broccoli Quiche

Prep Time: 10 minutes   Cook Time: 40 minutes

1 ½ cups milk
3 eggs
1 package KNORR® Recipe
   Classics™ Leek recipe mix
1 package (10 ounces) frozen
   chopped broccoli, thawed
   and drained
1 ½ cups shredded Cheddar, Swiss
   or Monterey Jack cheese
   (about 6 ounces)
1 (9-inch) unbaked or frozen
   deep-dish pie crust*

*If using 9-inch deep-dish frozen prepared
pie crust, do not thaw. Preheat oven and
cookie sheet. Pour filling into pie crust;
bake on cookie sheet.*

Makes 6 servings

• Preheat oven to 375°F. In large bowl, with fork, beat milk, eggs and recipe mix until blended. Stir in broccoli and cheese; spoon into pie crust.

• Bake 40 minutes or until knife inserted 1 inch from edge comes out clean. Let stand 10 minutes before serving.

Tip: Cheddar Broccoli Quiche accompanied with fresh fruit or cherry tomatoes is perfect for brunch or lunch. Or serve it with a mixed green salad and soup for a hearty dinner.

Pesto Turkey & Pasta

Prep Time: 10 minutes   Cook Time: 20 minutes

¼ cup milk
1 tablespoon margarine or butter
1 (4.7-ounce) package PASTA
   RONI® Chicken & Broccoli
   Flavor with Linguine
1 pound boneless, skinless turkey
   or chicken breasts, cut into
   thin strips
1 red or green bell pepper, sliced
½ medium onion, chopped
½ cup prepared pesto sauce
¼ cup pine nuts or chopped walnuts,
   toasted
   Grated Parmesan cheese (optional)

Makes 4 servings

1. In large saucepan, bring 1 ½ cups water, milk and margarine to a boil. Stir in pasta and Special Seasonings. Reduce heat to medium. Gently boil 1 minute.

2. Add turkey, bell pepper and onion. Return to a boil. Gently boil 8 to 9 minutes or until pasta is tender and turkey is no longer pink inside, stirring occasionally.

3. Stir in pesto. Let stand 3 to 5 minutes before serving. Sprinkle with nuts and cheese, if desired.

Tip: To make your own pesto, blend 2 cups fresh parsley or basil, 2 cloves garlic and ⅓ cup walnuts in a blender or food processor. Slowly add ½ cup olive oil and ¼ cup Parmesan cheese.

Cheddar Broccoli Quiche

Hearty Meatless Chili

1 envelope LIPTON® RECIPE SECRETS® Onion or Onion Mushroom Soup Mix
4 cups water
1 can (16 ounces) chick-peas, rinsed and drained
1 can (16 ounces) red kidney beans, rinsed and drained
1 can (14½ ounces) whole peeled tomatoes, undrained and chopped
1 cup lentils, rinsed and drained
1 large rib celery, coarsely chopped
1 tablespoon chili powder
2 teaspoons ground cumin (optional)
1 medium clove garlic, finely chopped

Makes about 4 (2-cup) servings

In 4-quart saucepan or stockpot, combine all ingredients. Bring to a boil over high heat. Reduce heat to low and simmer covered, stirring occasionally, 20 minutes or until lentils are almost tender. Remove cover and simmer, stirring occasionally, an additional 20 minutes or until liquid is almost absorbed and lentils are tender.

Note: For spicier chili, add ¼ teaspoon crushed red pepper flakes.

Serving Suggestion: Serve over hot cooked brown or white rice and top with shredded Cheddar cheese.

Shrimp and Pepper Noodle Bowl

2 packages (3 ounces each) shrimp-flavored instant ramen noodle soup mix
8 ounces frozen cooked medium shrimp, thawed
1 cup frozen bell pepper strips, cut into bite-size pieces
¼ cup chopped green onions
1 tablespoon soy sauce
½ teaspoon hot pepper sauce
2 tablespoons chopped cilantro

Makes 4 servings

1. Bring 4 cups water to a boil in large saucepan over high heat. Remove seasoning packets from noodles; set aside. Break up ramen noodles; add to water. Add shrimp and bell pepper; cook 3 minutes.

2. Add seasoning packets, green onions, soy sauce and hot pepper sauce; cook 1 minute. Garnish with cilantro.

Hearty Meatless Chili

Hidden Valley®
Broiled Fish

⅓ cup lemon juice
3 tablespoons olive oil
3 tablespoons dry white wine or
   water
1 packet (1 ounce) HIDDEN VALLEY®
   The Original Ranch® Salad
   Dressing & Seasoning Mix
1½ to 2 pounds mild white fish fillets,
   such as red snapper or sole

Makes 4 servings

Combine lemon juice, olive oil, wine and salad dressing
& seasoning mix in a shallow dish; mix well. Add fish and
coat all sides with mixture. Cover and refrigerate 15 to
30 minutes. Remove fish from marinade and place on
a broiler pan. Broil 9 to 12 minutes or until fish begins
to flake when tested with a fork.

Turkey Fettuccini

Prep Time: 30 minutes   Cook Time: 30 minutes

6 ounces regular or spinach
   fettuccini
1 cup frozen peas
1 (8-ounce) package white sauce
   mix
1¼ cups milk
¼ teaspoon nutmeg
2 cups JENNIE-O TURKEY STORE®
   Turkey Breast, cooked, cut into
   strips
⅓ cup Parmesan cheese, grated
1 (8-ounce) can sliced mushrooms
   (optional)

Prepare fettuccini and peas according to package
directions. Prepare white sauce according to package
directions using 1¼ cups milk; stir in nutmeg. Combine
hot drained fettuccini, peas, white sauce, turkey, cheese
and mushrooms, if desired. Toss to coat.

Hidden Valley® Broiled Fish

Pizza Meat Loaf

Makes 8 servings

1. Preheat oven to 350°F. In large bowl, combine all ingredients except ½ cup Pasta Sauce and ½ cup cheese.

2. In 13×9-inch baking or roasting pan, shape into loaf. Top with remaining ½ cup Pasta Sauce.

3. Bake uncovered 50 minutes.

4. Sprinkle top with remaining ½ cup cheese. Bake an additional 10 minutes or until done. Let stand 10 minutes before serving.

Tip: When grating cheese, spray your box grater with nonstick cooking spray and place on a sheet of waxed paper. When you finish grating, clean-up is a breeze. Simply discard the waxed paper and rinse the grater clean.

1 envelope LIPTON® RECIPE
   SECRETS® Onion Soup Mix*
2 pounds ground beef
1½ cups fresh bread crumbs
2 eggs
1 small green bell pepper, chopped
   (optional)
¼ cup water
1 cup RAGÚ® Old World Style®
   Pasta Sauce, divided
1 cup shredded mozzarella cheese
   (about 4 ounces), divided

Also terrific with LIPTON® RECIPE SECRETS® Savory Herb with Garlic Soup Mix.

White Chicken Chili

Prep Time: 10 minutes   Cook Time: 10 to 20 minutes

Makes 4 servings

In Dutch oven over medium-high heat, heat oil. Add onion; sauté 2 to 3 minutes or until softened and translucent. Add ground chicken; sauté 5 to 7 minutes or until no longer pink. Add chili seasoning mix and stir to combine. Add chicken broth and beans; bring to a boil. Reduce heat to medium-low; simmer 5 to 10 minutes or until all flavors are blended.

1 to 2 tablespoons canola oil
1 onion, chopped (about 1 cup)
1 package (about 1¼ pounds)
   PERDUE® Fresh Ground
   Chicken, Turkey or Turkey
   Breast Meat
1 package (about 1¾ ounces) chili
   seasoning mix
1 can (14½ ounces) reduced-sodium
   chicken broth
1 can (15 ounces) cannellini or
   white kidney beans,
   drained and rinsed

Pizza Meat Loaf

Baja Fish Tacos

½ cup sour cream
½ cup mayonnaise
¼ cup chopped fresh cilantro
1 package (1.25 ounces) ORTEGA®
    Taco Seasoning Mix, *divided*
1 pound (about 4) cod or other white
    fish fillets, cut into 1-inch pieces
2 tablespoons vegetable oil
2 tablespoons lemon juice
1 package (12) ORTEGA Taco Shells

TOPPINGS
    Shredded cabbage, chopped
        tomato, lime juice, ORTEGA
        Taco Sauce

Makes 6 servings

COMBINE sour cream, mayonnaise, cilantro and *2 tablespoons* taco seasoning mix in small bowl.

COMBINE cod, vegetable oil, lemon juice and *remaining* taco seasoning mix in medium bowl; pour into large skillet. Cook, stirring constantly, over medium-high heat for 4 to 5 minutes or until fish flakes easily when tested with fork.

FILL taco shells with fish mixture. Layer with desired toppings. Top with sour cream sauce.

Tip: Try a variety of fish and seafood such as shark, shrimp, crab or lobster in these fresh-tasting tacos.

Onion-Baked Pork Chops

1 envelope LIPTON® RECIPE
    SECRETS® Golden Onion
    Soup Mix*
⅓ cup plain dry bread crumbs
4 pork chops, 1 inch thick
    (about 3 pounds)
1 egg, well beaten

*Also terrific with LIPTON® RECIPE SECRETS® Onion or Savory Herb with Garlic Soup Mix.

Makes 4 servings

1. Preheat oven to 400°F. In small bowl, combine soup mix and bread crumbs. Dip pork chops in egg, then bread crumb mixture until evenly coated.

2. On baking sheet, arrange pork chops.

3. Bake uncovered 20 minutes or until done, turning once.

Baja Fish Tacos

Country Roasted Chicken Dinner

1 envelope LIPTON® RECIPE
   SECRETS® Savory Herb
   with Garlic Soup Mix*
2 tablespoons honey
1 tablespoon water
1 tablespoon I CAN'T BELIEVE IT'S
   NOT BUTTER!® Spread, melted
1 roasting chicken (5 to 6 pounds)
3 pounds all-purpose and/or sweet
   potatoes, cut into chunks

*Also terrific with LIPTON® RECIPE
SECRETS® Golden Herb with Lemon
or Golden Onion Soup Mix.

Makes about 8 servings

1. Preheat oven to 350°F.

2. In small bowl, blend soup mix, honey, water and I Can't Believe It's Not Butter!® Spread.

3. In 18×12-inch roasting pan, arrange chicken, breast side up; brush with soup mixture. Cover loosely with aluminum foil. Roast 30 minutes; drain off drippings. Arrange potatoes around chicken and continue roasting covered, stirring potatoes occasionally, 1 hour or until meat thermometer reaches 175°F and potatoes are tender. *If chicken reaches 175°F before potatoes are tender, remove chicken to serving platter and keep warm. Continue roasting potatoes until tender.*

Note: Insert meat thermometer into thickest part of thigh between breast and thigh. Make sure tip does not touch bone.

Serving Suggestion: Serve with a mixed green salad, warm biscuits and Lipton® Iced Tea.

quick tip

Whole chickens range in size from about 2½ to 10 pounds. The smallest, called frying chickens (also called broiler-fryers or broilers), are the most common; they are intended for frying and broiling but can also be used for braising, poaching, baking and grilling. Larger chickens are called roasters, weighing from 2½ to 5 pounds or more. Somewhat older than fryers, these birds have more fat, making them well suited to oven roasting.

Country Roasted Chicken Dinner

Classic Fajitas

1 beef flank or skirt steak
(1½ pounds)
2 large onions, cut into ½-inch slices
2 medium green bell peppers, cut
into quarters
12 small flour tortillas (6- to 7-inch
diameter), warmed
Salt and pepper
Prepared guacamole (optional)

MARINADE:
1 package (about 1.25 ounces)
fajita seasoning mix
¼ cup water
2 tablespoons fresh lime juice

Makes 6 servings

1. Combine marinade ingredients in small bowl. Place beef steak and marinade in food-safe plastic bag; turn steak to coat. Close bag securely and marinate in refrigerator 6 hours or as long as overnight, turning occasionally.

2. Remove steak from marinade; discard marinade. Place steak in center of grid over medium, ash-covered coals; arrange onions and bell peppers around steak. Grill flank steak, uncovered, 17 to 21 minutes (skirt steak 10 to 13 minutes) for medium rare to medium doneness, turning occasionally. Grill vegetables 13 to 16 minutes or until crisp-tender, turning occasionally.

3. Carve flank steak lengthwise in half, then crosswise into thin slices. (Carve skirt steak diagonally across the grain into thin slices.) Cut bell peppers into ½-inch strips; coarsely chop onions. Place steak slices on tortillas; top with vegetables. Season with salt and pepper, as desired. Serve with guacamole, if desired.

Tip: Wrap tortillas in heavy-duty foil and place on grid over medium, ash-covered coals. Grill 5 minutes or until warm, turning occasionally. Keep warm until ready to serve.

Favorite recipe from **National Cattlemen's Beef Association on behalf of The Beef Checkoff**

Classic Fajitas

Onion-Apple Glazed Pork Tenderloin

Prep Time: 5 minutes   Cook Time: 25 minutes

1 (1½- to 2-pound) boneless pork
    tenderloin
  Black pepper
2 tablespoons BERTOLLI® Olive Oil,
    divided
1 envelope LIPTON® RECIPE
    SECRETS® Onion Soup Mix
½ cup apple juice
2 tablespoons firmly packed brown
    sugar
¾ cup water
¼ cup dry red wine or water
1 tablespoon all-purpose flour

Makes 4 to 6 servings

1. Preheat oven to 425°F. In small roasting pan or baking pan, arrange pork. Season with pepper and rub with 1 tablespoon olive oil. Roast uncovered 10 minutes.

2. Meanwhile, in small bowl, combine remaining 1 tablespoon olive oil, soup mix, apple juice and brown sugar. Pour over pork and continue roasting 10 minutes or until desired doneness. Remove pork to serving platter; cover with aluminum foil.

3. Place roasting pan over medium-high heat and bring pan juices to a boil, scraping up browned bits from bottom of pan. Stir in water, wine and flour; boil, stirring constantly, 1 minute or until thickened.

4. To serve, thinly slice pork and serve with gravy.

Black and White Chili

Prep and Cook Time: 30 minutes

  Nonstick cooking spray
1 pound chicken tenders, cut into
    ¾-inch pieces
1 cup coarsely chopped onion
1 can (15½ ounces) Great Northern
    beans, rinsed and drained
1 can (15 ounces) black beans,
    rinsed and drained
1 can (about 14 ounces) Mexican-
    style stewed tomatoes,
    undrained
2 tablespoons Texas-style chili
    powder seasoning mix

Makes 6 servings

1. Spray large saucepan with cooking spray; heat over medium heat. Add chicken and onion; cook and stir over medium-high heat 5 to 8 minutes or until chicken is browned.

2. Stir beans, tomatoes with juice and seasoning mix into saucepan; bring to a boil. Reduce heat to low; simmer, uncovered, 10 minutes.

Serving Suggestion: Serve the chili over cooked rice or pasta.

Onion-Apple Glazed Pork Tenderloin

Southern Pecan Cornbread Stuffing *(page 160)*

oh-so-easy
side dishes

Cheddary Mashed Potato Bake

Prep Time: 5 minutes   Cook Time: 10 minutes

Makes 8 servings

1 box (7.2 ounces) roasted garlic mashed potato mix
1 cup sour cream
1 ½ cups shredded Cheddar cheese, divided
1 ½ cups **French's**® Cheddar French Fried Onions

1. Preheat oven to 375°F. Prepare potatoes as directed on package for 2 pouches (8 servings). Stir in sour cream and 1 cup cheese. Heat through.

2. Spoon mixture into 2-quart baking dish. Sprinkle with remaining ½ cup cheese and French Fried Onions. Bake 10 minutes until hot and golden.

Southern Pecan Cornbread Stuffing

Prep Time: 5 minutes   Cook Time: 35 minutes

Makes 8 servings

5 cups dry cornbread stuffing mix
1 package KNORR® Recipe Classics™ Leek recipe mix
½ cup (1 stick) I CAN'T BELIEVE IT'S NOT BUTTER!® Spread
1 cup coarsely chopped pecans
1 package (10 ounces) frozen corn, thawed and drained
1 cup hot water
1 cup orange juice

• Preheat oven to 350°F. In large bowl, combine stuffing and recipe mix.

• In 8-inch skillet, melt I Can't Believe It's Not Butter!® Spread over medium heat and cook pecans, stirring occasionally, 5 minutes.

• Add corn, water, orange juice and pecan mixture to stuffing; toss until moistened. Spoon into 2-quart casserole sprayed with nonstick cooking spray.

• Cover and bake 30 minutes or until heated through.

Cheddary Mashed Potato Bake

Grilled Mesquite Vegetables

Prep Time: 10 minutes   Cook Time: 10 minutes

2 to 3 tablespoons MRS. DASH®
     Mesquite Grilling Blend
2 tablespoons olive oil, divided
1 eggplant, trimmed and cut into
     ½-inch slices
1 zucchini, quartered lengthwise
1 red onion, peeled and halved
2 red bell peppers, cut into large
     slices
2 green bell peppers, cut into large
     slices
1 tablespoon balsamic vinegar

Makes 6 servings

Preheat barbecue grill to medium. In large bowl, combine Mrs. Dash® Mesquite Grilling Blend and 1 tablespoon olive oil. Add vegetables and toss until well coated. Place vegetables on grill. Cover and cook, turning vegetables once during cooking, until vegetables are tender and develop grill marks, about 3 to 4 minutes on each side. Remove vegetables from grill as soon as they are cooked. Coarsely chop vegetables into ½-inch pieces. Mix remaining olive oil and balsamic vinegar in large bowl. Add cut vegetables and toss to coat. Serve at room temperature.

Note: Grilling vegetables dehydrates them slightly and intensifies flavors while Mrs. Dash® Mesquite Grilling Blend adds a third dimension of flavor. This dish makes a colorful accompaniment to any grilled meat.

Southwestern Rice

1 cup uncooked converted rice
1 can (15 ounces) black beans,
     rinsed and drained
1 can (8 ounces) corn, drained
1 packet (1 ounce) HIDDEN VALLEY®
     The Original Ranch® Salad
     Dressing & Seasoning Mix
¾ cup (3 ounces) diced Monterey
     Jack cheese
½ cup diced seeded tomato
¼ cup sliced green onions

Makes 6 servings

Cook rice according to package directions, omitting salt. During last 5 minutes of cooking time, quickly uncover and add beans and corn; cover immediately. When rice is done, remove saucepan from heat; stir in salad dressing & seasoning mix. Let stand 5 minutes. Stir in cheese, tomato and onions. Serve immediately.

Grilled Mesquite Vegetables

Tomato Cheese Bread

1 can (14.5 ounces) CONTADINA®
  Recipe Ready Diced Tomatoes
2 cups buttermilk baking mix
2 teaspoons dried oregano leaves,
  crushed, divided
¾ cup (3 ounces) shredded Cheddar
  cheese
¾ cup (3 ounces) shredded Monterey
  Jack cheese

Makes 12 servings

1. Drain tomatoes, reserving juice.

2. Combine baking mix, 1 teaspoon oregano and ⅔ cup reserved tomato juice in medium bowl.

3. Press dough evenly to edges of 11×7×2-inch greased baking dish. Sprinkle with Cheddar cheese and remaining oregano. Distribute tomato pieces evenly over Cheddar cheese; sprinkle with Jack cheese.

4. Bake in preheated 375°F oven 25 minutes or until edges are golden brown and cheese is bubbly. Cool 5 minutes before cutting into squares to serve.

Cheesy Baked Potatoes
Prep Time: 15 minutes   Cook Time: 50 minutes

1 package (32 ounces) frozen hash
  brown potatoes, divided
2 cups milk
1 package (1.3 ounces) tomato
  cream pasta sauce mix
2 cups (8 ounces) shredded
  Cheddar-Monterey Jack cheese,
  divided
¼ cup **French's**® Honey Dijon
  Mustard
3 green onions, chopped

Makes 10 servings

1. Preheat oven to 400°F. Spray 13×9-inch baking dish with nonstick cooking spray. Sprinkle half of potatoes in baking dish.

2. Combine milk and sauce mix in medium saucepan. Bring to a boil. Reduce heat; cook 4 minutes or until slightly thickened, stirring often. Remove from heat. Add 1 cup cheese, mustard and green onions; stir until cheese melts. Pour half of sauce over potatoes. Repeat layers with remaining potatoes and sauce. Cover tightly with foil.

3. Bake 50 minutes or until center is heated through. Uncover; stir. Top with remaining cheese.

TIP: Casserole may be baked in disposable foil pan. To reheat, cover and place on grill over low heat until heated through.

Tomato Cheese Bread

Stovetop Summer Squash

1⅔ cups water
1 package (6 ounces) stuffing mix with herb seasoning packet
3 tablespoons butter
1 cup chopped onion
1 cup chopped red bell pepper
1 tablespoon minced fresh basil
2 cups sliced yellow squash
2 cups sliced zucchini

Makes 6 servings

1. Bring water to a boil in 2-quart saucepan. Add seasoning packet from stuffing mix; cover and cook 15 minutes over low heat.

2. Meanwhile, melt butter in large skillet over medium heat. Add onion and bell pepper; cook and stir 3 minutes or until tender. Add basil, squash and zucchini; cook and stir 3 minutes or until vegetables are tender.

3. Transfer squash mixture to saucepan with seasoning blend. Add stuffing croutons; mix until all liquid is absorbed. Remove from heat; cover and let stand 5 minutes. Fluff with fork before serving.

Homestyle Spinach and Mushrooms

1 packet (1 ounce) HIDDEN VALLEY® The Original Ranch® Salad Dressing & Seasoning Mix
1 cup milk
1 cup mayonnaise
2 boxes (10 ounces *each*) frozen chopped spinach, cooked and well-drained
1 jar (4.5 ounces) sliced mushrooms, drained
½ cup shredded Parmesan cheese
1 cup crushed croutons, for topping

Makes 4 to 6 servings

In a bowl, combine salad dressing & seasoning mix with milk and mayonnaise. Mix well. Cover and refrigerate. Chill 30 minutes to thicken. Combine dressing with remaining ingredients, except croutons, in a 9-inch square baking dish. Top with croutons. Bake at 325°F for 25 minutes or until thoroughly heated.

Stovetop Summer Squash

1 envelope LIPTON® RECIPE
   SECRETS® Onion Soup Mix*
4 medium all-purpose potatoes,
   cut into large chunks
   (about 2 pounds)
⅓ cup BERTOLLI® Olive Oil

*Also terrific with LIPTON® RECIPE
SECRETS® Onion Mushroom, Golden
Onion or Savory Herb with Garlic
Soup Mix.*

Onion-Roasted Potatoes

Prep Time: 10 minutes   Cook Time: 40 minutes

Makes 4 servings

1. Preheat oven to 450°F. In 13×9-inch baking or roasting pan, combine all ingredients.

2. Bake uncovered, stirring occasionally, 40 minutes or until potatoes are tender and golden brown.

1 pound BOB EVANS® Zesty Hot
   Roll Sausage
3 cups all-purpose (biscuit)
   baking mix
1¼ cups (5 ounces) shredded sharp
   Cheddar cheese
1 cup seeded diced fresh or drained
   canned tomatoes
1 cup chopped green onions
1 cup milk
¼ teaspoon paprika
   Dash cayenne pepper
   Butter (optional)

Southwestern Sausage Drop Biscuits

Makes about 2 dozen small biscuits

Preheat oven to 350°F. Crumble and cook sausage in medium skillet until browned. Drain on paper towels. Combine sausage and remaining ingredients except butter in large bowl; mix well. Shape dough into 2-inch balls; place on ungreased baking sheet. Bake 12 minutes or until golden. Serve hot with butter, if desired. Refrigerate leftovers.

Onion-Roasted Potatoes

¼ pound spicy sausage, crumbled
½ medium onion, chopped
1 stalk celery, sliced
1 package (6 ounces) wild and long
    grain rice seasoned mix
1 can (14½ ounces) DEL MONTE®
    Stewed Tomatoes - Original
    Recipe
½ green bell pepper, chopped
¼ cup chopped parsley

2 cups milk
1 package KNORR® Recipe
    Classics™ Leek recipe mix
1 bag (16 ounces) frozen chopped
    spinach
⅛ teaspoon ground nutmeg

Bayou Dirty Rice
Prep & Cook Time: 40 minutes

Makes 4 to 6 servings

1. Brown sausage and onion in large skillet over medium-high heat; drain. Add celery, rice and seasoning packet; cook and stir 2 minutes.

2. Drain tomatoes, reserving liquid; pour liquid into measuring cup. Add water to measure 1⅓ cups; pour over rice. Add tomatoes; bring to boil. Cover and cook over low heat 20 minutes. Add bell pepper and parsley.

3. Cover and cook 5 minutes or until rice is tender. Serve with roasted chicken or Cornish game hens.

Creamed Spinach
Prep Time: 5 minutes   Cook Time: 10 minutes

Makes 6 servings

• In medium saucepan, combine milk and recipe mix. Bring to a boil over medium heat.

• Add spinach and nutmeg; stirring frequently. Bring to a boil over high heat. Reduce heat to low and simmer, stirring frequently, 5 minutes.

Bayou Dirty Rice

1 package (8½ ounces) corn muffin
    mix
1 can (11 ounces) Mexican-style
    corn, drained
½ cup HELLMANN'S® or BEST
    FOODS® Real Mayonnaise
1 egg, slightly beaten

Super-Moist Cornbread

Prep Time: 5 Minutes   Cook Time: 25 Minutes

Makes 8 servings

1. Preheat oven to 400°F. Spray 8-inch round cake pan with nonstick cooking spray; set aside.

2. In medium bowl combine all ingredients until moistened. Evenly spread into prepared pan.

3. Bake 25 minutes or until toothpick inserted in center comes out clean.

1 pound lean ground beef
1 can (28 ounces) whole peeled
    tomatoes, undrained
2 cans (15½ ounces each) chili
    beans
1 cup chopped onions
1 cup water
1 packet (1 ounce) HIDDEN VALLEY®
    The Original Ranch® Salad
    Dressing & Seasoning Mix
1 teaspoon chili powder
1 bay leaf

Texas Ranch Chili Beans

Makes 8 servings

In a Dutch oven, brown beef over medium-high heat; drain off fat. Add tomatoes, breaking up with a spoon. Stir in beans, onions, water, salad dressing & seasoning mix, chili powder and bay leaf. Bring to boil; reduce heat and simmer, uncovered, 1 hour, stirring occasionally. Remove bay leaf just before serving.

Super-Moist Cornbread

Easy Fried Rice

Prep Time: 10 minutes   Cook Time: 10 minutes

¼ cup BERTOLLI® Olive Oil
4 cups cooked rice
2 cloves garlic, finely chopped
1 envelope LIPTON® RECIPE
    SECRETS® Onion Mushroom
    Soup Mix
½ cup water
1 tablespoon soy sauce
1 cup frozen peas and carrots,
    partially thawed
2 eggs, lightly beaten

Makes 4 servings

1. In 12-inch nonstick skillet, heat oil over medium-high heat and cook rice, stirring constantly, 2 minutes or until rice is heated through. Stir in garlic.

2. Stir in soup mix blended with water and soy sauce and cook 1 minute. Stir in peas and carrots and cook 2 minutes or until heated through.

3. Make a well in center of rice and quickly stir in eggs until cooked.

Spinach Spoonbread

1 package frozen onions in cream
    sauce
1 (10-ounce) package frozen
    chopped spinach
1 (8-ounce) package corn muffin mix
1 cup CABOT® Sour Cream
½ cup grated CABOT® Cheddar
    (about 2 ounces)
2 large eggs, lightly beaten
¼ teaspoon salt

Makes 4 servings

1. Preheat oven to 350°F. Butter 1½-quart baking dish or coat with nonstick cooking spray and set aside.

2. Prepare onions according to package directions. Cook spinach according to package directions and drain well.

3. In large bowl, combine onions and spinach with remaining ingredients, mixing thoroughly. Transfer mixture to prepared dish.

4. Bake for 30 to 35 minutes.

Easy Fried Rice

Apple Pecan Stuffing

½ cup butter
1 large onion, chopped
1 large Granny Smith apple, peeled and diced
2½ cups chicken broth
1 package (16 ounces) cornbread stuffing mix
½ cup chopped pecans, toasted

Makes 10 to 12 servings

1. Preheat oven to 325°F. Melt butter in large saucepan. Add onion; cook 5 minutes, stirring occasionally. Add apple; cook 1 minute. Add chicken broth; bring to a simmer. Remove from heat; stir in stuffing mix and pecans.

2. If desired, loosely fill cavity of turkey with stuffing just before roasting. Place remaining stuffing in ovenproof casserole dish. Cover and bake 45 minutes or until hot. (Or, stuffing may be baked at 375°F 30 minutes while turkey is standing.)

Note: Stuffing may be prepared up to 1 day before serving (store covered and refrigerated). Let stand at room temperature 30 minutes before baking or stuffing turkey.

Hidden Valley® Glazed Baby Carrots

¼ cup butter
¼ cup packed light brown sugar
1 package (16 ounces) ready-to-eat baby carrots, cooked
1 packet (1 ounce) HIDDEN VALLEY® The Original Ranch® Salad Dressing & Seasoning Mix

Makes 4 to 6 servings

Melt butter and sugar in a large skillet. Add carrots and salad dressing & seasoning mix; stir well. Cook over medium heat until carrots are tender and glazed, about 5 minutes, stirring frequently.

Apple Pecan Stuffing

Savory Skillet Broccoli

Prep Time: 5 minutes   Cook Time: 10 minutes

1 tablespoon BERTOLLI® Olive Oil
6 cups fresh broccoli florets *or*
    1 pound green beans, trimmed
1 envelope LIPTON® RECIPE
    SECRETS® Golden Onion
    Soup Mix*
1½ cups water

Also terrific with LIPTON® RECIPE SECRETS® Onion Mushroom Soup Mix.

Makes 4 servings

1. In 12-inch skillet, heat oil over medium-high heat and cook broccoli, stirring occasionally, 2 minutes.

2. Stir in soup mix blended with water. Bring to a boil over high heat.

3. Reduce heat to medium-low and simmer covered 6 minutes or until broccoli is tender.

Louisiana Red Beans & Rice

1 package (7.2 ounces)
    RICE-A-RONI® Herb & Butter
1 cup chopped green or yellow
    bell pepper
¾ cup chopped onion
2 cloves garlic, minced
2 tablespoons vegetable oil or
    olive oil
1 can (15 or 16 ounces) red beans
    or kidney beans, rinsed and
    drained
1 can (14½ or 16 ounces) tomatoes
    or stewed tomatoes, undrained
1 teaspoon dried thyme leaves or
    dried oregano leaves
⅛ teaspoon hot pepper sauce or
    black pepper
2 tablespoons chopped parsley
    (optional)

Makes 5 servings

1. Prepare Rice-A-Roni® Mix as package directs.

2. While Rice-A-Roni® is simmering, in large skillet, sauté green pepper, onion and garlic in oil 5 minutes.

3. Stir in beans, tomatoes, thyme and hot pepper sauce. Simmer, uncovered, 10 minutes, stirring occasionally. Stir in parsley. Serve over rice.

Serving Suggestion: Serve with one 8-ounce glass of milk per serving.

Savory Skillet Broccoli

Pizza Biscuits

2½ cups baking mix
1 cup CABOT® Sour Cream
4 ounces CABOT® Sharp Cheddar, grated (1 cup)
½ cup chopped cooked ham

1. Preheat oven to 400°F.

2. In mixing bowl, combine baking mix, sour cream, cheese and ham; stir together to form soft dough.

3. Turn dough out onto lightly floured work surface and pat into ¾-inch-thick layer. Cut out biscuits with cutter. Place on baking sheet.

4. Bake for 12 to 15 minutes or until golden brown; serve hot.

Holiday Wild Rice Pilaf

Prep Time: 8 minutes   Cooking Time: 28 minutes

2 tablespoons butter or margarine
½ cup chopped onion
½ cup sliced celery
1 can (14½ ounces) low-salt chicken broth
½ cup water
1 package (6 ounces) original flavor long grain and wild rice mix
¾ cup SUN-MAID® Raisins or Goldens & Cherries
⅓ cup coarsely chopped pecans, toasted

Makes 4 to 6 servings (about 4½ cups)

MELT butter in medium saucepan or skillet over medium-high heat.

ADD onion and celery; cook 3 minutes, stirring occasionally.

ADD broth, water, rice, contents of seasoning packet and fruit. Bring to a boil. Reduce heat to medium-low. Cover and simmer 25 minutes or until liquid is absorbed.

STIR in pecans.

Tip: The pilaf makes a wonderful stuffing for turkey or chicken.

Pizza Biscuits

Garlic Mashed Potatoes

6 medium all-purpose potatoes, peeled, if desired, and cut into chunks (about 3 pounds)
Water
1 envelope LIPTON® RECIPE SECRETS® Savory Herb with Garlic Soup Mix*
½ cup milk
½ cup I CAN'T BELIEVE IT'S NOT BUTTER!® Spread

Also terrific with LIPTON® RECIPE SECRETS® Onion or Golden Onion Soup Mix.

Makes 8 servings

1. In 4-quart saucepan, cover potatoes with water; bring to a boil.

2. Reduce heat to low and simmer uncovered 20 minutes or until potatoes are very tender; drain.

3. Return potatoes to saucepan, then mash. Stir in remaining ingredients.

Savory Rosemary Quick Bread

Prep Time: 15 minutes   Cook Time: 21 minutes

1¾ cups reduced-fat buttermilk baking mix
1 cup (4 ounces) shredded Cheddar cheese, divided
¾ cup skim milk
2 egg whites
1⅓ cups **French's**® French Fried Onions, divided
1 tablespoon sugar
1 tablespoon butter, melted
2 teaspoons chopped fresh rosemary *or* ½ teaspoon dried rosemary

Makes 8 servings

1. Preheat oven to 375°F. Line 9-inch square baking pan with foil; spray with nonstick cooking spray.

2. Combine baking mix, ½ cup cheese, milk, egg whites, ⅔ *cup* French Fried Onions, sugar, butter and rosemary in large bowl; stir just until moistened. *Do not overmix.* Spread into prepared pan.

3. Bake 20 minutes or until toothpick inserted in center comes out clean. Sprinkle with remaining cheese and ⅔ cup onions. Bake 1 minute or until cheese is melted and onions are golden. Remove to wire rack; cool 5 minutes. Remove foil. Cut into squares. Serve warm or cool.

Garlic Mashed Potatoes

Oniony Corn Spoonbread

Prep Time: 5 minutes   Cook Time: 45 minutes

1 can (14¾ ounces) cream-style corn
1 can (11 ounces) Mexican-style corn
1 cup sour cream
1 package (6½ to 8½ ounces) corn muffin mix
½ cup diced red and green bell pepper
1 large egg
2 tablespoons butter or margarine, melted
1⅓ cups **French's®** French Fried Onions, divided
½ cup (2 ounces) shredded Cheddar cheese
   Red bell pepper and chopped parsley (optional)

Makes 8 servings

1. Preheat oven to 350°F. Combine corn, sour cream, corn muffin mix, bell peppers, egg, butter and ⅔ *cup* French Fried Onions. Pour mixture into greased shallow 2-quart baking dish.

2. Bake 40 minutes or until set. Top with cheese and remaining ⅔ *cup* onions; bake 5 minutes or until onions are golden. Garnish with bell pepper and parsley, if desired.

Variation: For added Cheddar flavor, substitute **French's®** Cheddar French Fried Onions for the original flavor.

Hash Brown Bake

1 packet (1 ounce) HIDDEN VALLEY® The Original Ranch® Salad Dressing & Seasoning Mix
1¼ cups milk
3 ounces cream cheese
6 cups hash browns (frozen shredded potatoes)
1 tablespoon bacon bits
½ cup shredded sharp Cheddar cheese

Makes 4 servings

In a blender, combine salad dressing & seasoning mix, milk and cream cheese. Pour over potatoes and bacon bits in a 9-inch square baking dish. Top with cheese. Bake at 350°F for 35 minutes.

Oniony Corn Spoonbread

Peach Cream Cake *(page 288)*

almost homemade

cakes

Angel Almond Cupcakes

1 package DUNCAN HINES®
  Angel Food Cake Mix
1¼ cups water
2 teaspoons almond extract
1 container DUNCAN HINES®
  Wild Cherry Vanilla Frosting

Makes 30 to 32 cupcakes

1. Preheat oven to 350°F.

2. Combine cake mix, water and almond extract in large bowl. Beat at low speed with electric mixer until moistened. Beat at medium speed for 1 minute. Line medium muffin pans with paper baking cups. Fill muffin cups two-thirds full. Bake at 350°F for 20 to 25 minutes or until golden brown, cracked and dry on top. Remove from muffin pans. Cool completely. Frost with frosting.

Peach Cream Cake

1 (10¾-ounce) loaf angel food cake, frozen
1 (14-ounce) can EAGLE BRAND®
  Sweetened Condensed Milk
  (NOT evaporated milk)
1 cup cold water
1 teaspoon almond extract
1 (4-serving-size) package instant vanilla pudding mix
2 cups (1 pint) whipping cream, whipped
4 cups sliced peeled fresh peaches (about 2 pounds)

Makes one (13×9-inch) cake

1. Cut cake into ¼-inch slices; arrange half the slices on bottom of ungreased 13×9-inch baking dish.

2. In large bowl, combine EAGLE BRAND®, water and almond extract. Add pudding mix; beat well. Chill 5 minutes.

3. Fold in whipped cream. Spread half the cream mixture over cake slices; arrange half the peach slices on top. Top with remaining cake slices, cream filling and peach slices.

4. Chill 4 hours or until set. Cut into squares to serve. Store leftovers covered in refrigerator.

Angel Almond Cupcakes

Orange Glow Bundt Cake

1 (18.25-ounce) package moist yellow cake mix, plus ingredients to prepare mix
1 tablespoon grated orange peel
1 cup orange juice
¼ cup sugar
1 tablespoon TABASCO® brand Pepper Sauce
1¾ cups confectioners' sugar

Makes 12 servings

Preheat oven to 375°F. Grease 12-cup bundt pan. Prepare cake mix according to package directions, adding orange peel to batter. Bake 35 to 40 minutes or until toothpick inserted in center of cake comes out clean.

Meanwhile, heat orange juice, sugar and TABASCO® Sauce to boiling in 1-quart saucepan. Reduce heat to low; simmer, uncovered, 5 minutes. Remove from heat. Reserve ¼ cup orange juice mixture for glaze.

Remove cake from oven. With wooden skewer, poke holes in cake (in pan) in several places. Spoon remaining orange juice mixture over cake. Cool cake in pan 10 minutes. Carefully invert cake onto wire rack to cool completely.

Combine reserved ¼ cup orange juice mixture and confectioners' sugar in small bowl until smooth. Place cake on platter; spoon glaze over cake. Garnish with mint leaves and orange slices, if desired.

quick tip

When the peel will be used, scrub the orange thoroughly to remove any pesticide residues as well as the wax coating. The peel can be grated with the fine side of a box grater. One medium orange yields ⅓ to ½ cup juice and 1 to 2 tablespoons grated peel.

Orange Glow Bundt Cake

Chocolate Tiramisu Cupcakes

CUPCAKES
1 package (18¼ ounces) chocolate
    cake mix
1¼ cups water
3 eggs
⅓ cup vegetable oil or melted butter
2 tablespoons instant espresso
    powder
2 tablespoons brandy (optional)

FROSTING
8 ounces mascarpone cheese or
    cream cheese
1½ to 1¾ cups powdered sugar
2 tablespoons coffee-flavored liqueur
1 tablespoon unsweetened cocoa
    powder

Makes 30 cupcakes

1. Preheat oven to 350°F. Line 30 standard (2½-inch) muffin pan cups with paper baking cups.

2. Combine all cupcake ingredients in large bowl; beat with electric mixer at low speed 30 seconds. Beat at medium speed 2 minutes.

3. Spoon batter into prepared muffin cups, filling two-thirds full. Bake 20 to 22 minutes or until toothpick inserted into centers comes out clean. Cool in pans on wire racks 10 minutes. Remove to wire racks; cool completely. (At this point, cupcakes may be frozen up to 3 months. Thaw at room temperature before frosting.)

4. For frosting, combine mascarpone cheese and 1½ cups powdered sugar in large bowl; beat with electric mixer at medium speed until well blended. Add liqueur; beat until well blended. If frosting is too soft, beat in additional powdered sugar or chill until spreadable.

5. Frost cooled cupcakes with frosting. Place cocoa in strainer; shake over cupcakes. Store at room temperature up to 24 hours or cover and refrigerate for up to 3 days before serving.

Chocolate Tiramisu Cupcakes

Flower Power Strawberry Cake

1 package (18¼ ounces) white cake
   mix *without* pudding in the mix
2 containers (6 ounces each)
   strawberry yogurt
4 eggs
⅓ cup vegetable oil
1 package (4-serving size)
   strawberry gelatin
1 container (8 ounces) frozen
   whipped topping, thawed,
   divided
12 to 13 medium strawberries, hulled
   Yellow food coloring

Makes 15 servings

1. Preheat oven to 350°F. Lightly grease 13×9-inch baking pan.

2. Beat cake mix, yogurt, eggs, oil and gelatin in large bowl with electric mixer at low speed about 1 minute or until blended. Increase speed to medium; beat 1 to 2 minutes or until smooth. Spread batter in prepared pan.

3. Bake 38 to 43 minutes or until toothpick inserted into center comes out clean. Cool completely in pan on wire rack.

4. Reserve ½ cup whipped topping in small bowl. Spread remaining topping over cooled cake. Cut each strawberry lengthwise into 6 wedges. Use strawberry wedges to create 15 flowers on top of cake. For each flower, place 5 strawberry wedges, pointed ends towards center, to create flower petals as shown in photo.

5. Tint reserved whipped topping with 6 to 8 drops yellow food coloring. Place tinted topping in resealable food storage bag; cut off ⅛ inch from corner of bag. Pipe yellow whipped topping into center of each flower. Serve cake immediately or loosely cover and refrigerate for up to 24 hours.

Flower Power Strawberry Cake

Raspberry Buckle Cupcakes

½ (18-ounce) package refrigerated sugar cookie dough*
½ cup all-purpose flour
¼ cup firmly packed brown sugar
1 teaspoon vanilla
½ cup slivered almonds
1 package (18¼ ounces) lemon cake mix, plus ingredients to prepare mix
1 can (12 ounces) raspberry pie filling

*Save remaining ½ package of dough for another use.

Makes 24 cupcakes

1. Preheat oven to 350°F. Line 24 standard (2½-inch) muffin pan cups with paper or foil baking cups.

2. For topping, combine cookie dough, flour, brown sugar and vanilla in large bowl; beat until well blended. Stir in almonds.

3. Prepare cake mix according to package directions. Divide batter evenly among prepared muffin pan cups; top batter with 1 tablespoon pie filling. Bake 10 minutes.

4. Sprinkle topping evenly over partially baked cupcakes. Bake 15 minutes or until topping is brown and cupcakes are set.

Pumpkin Crunch Cake

1 package (18.25 ounces) yellow cake mix, *divided*
1⅔ cups LIBBY'S® Easy Pumpkin Pie Mix
2 large eggs
2 teaspoons pumpkin pie spice
⅓ cup flaked coconut
¼ cup chopped nuts
3 tablespoons butter or margarine, softened

Makes 20 servings

PREHEAT oven to 350°F. Grease 13×9-inch baking pan.

COMBINE *3 cups* yellow cake mix, pumpkin pie mix, eggs and pumpkin pie spice in large mixer bowl. Beat on medium speed of electric mixer for 2 minutes. Pour into prepared baking pan.

COMBINE *remaining* cake mix, coconut and nuts in small bowl; cut in butter with pastry blender or two knives until mixture is crumbly. Sprinkle over batter.

BAKE for 30 to 35 minutes or until wooden pick inserted in center comes out clean. Cool in pan on wire rack.

Raspberry Buckle Cupcakes

Fudge Ribbon Cake

Prep Time: 20 minutes   Bake Time: 40 minutes

1 (18.25- or 18.5-ounce) package chocolate cake mix
1 (8-ounce) package cream cheese, softened
2 tablespoons butter or margarine, softened
1 tablespoon cornstarch
1 (14-ounce) can EAGLE BRAND® Sweetened Condensed Milk (NOT evaporated milk)
1 egg
1 teaspoon vanilla extract
Chocolate Glaze (recipe follows)

Makes 10 to 12 servings

1. Preheat oven to 350°F. Grease and flour 13×9-inch baking pan. Prepare cake mix as package directs. Pour batter into prepared pan.

2. In small bowl, beat cream cheese, butter and cornstarch until fluffy. Gradually beat in EAGLE BRAND®. Add egg and vanilla; beat until smooth. Spoon evenly over cake batter.

3. Bake 40 minutes or until toothpick inserted near center comes out clean. Cool. Drizzle with Chocolate Glaze. Store leftovers covered in refrigerator.

Chocolate Glaze: In small saucepan, over low heat, melt 1 (1-ounce) square unsweetened or semisweet chocolate and 1 tablespoon butter or margarine with 2 tablespoons water. Remove from heat. Stir in ¾ cup confectioners' sugar and ½ teaspoon vanilla extract. Stir until smooth and well blended. Makes about ⅓ cup glaze.

Fudge Ribbon Bundt Cake: Preheat oven to 350°F. Grease and flour 10-inch Bundt pan. Prepare cake mix as package directs. Pour batter into prepared pan. Prepare cream cheese layer as directed above; spoon evenly over batter. Bake 50 to 55 minutes or until toothpick inserted near center comes out clean. Cool 10 minutes. Remove from pan. Cool. Prepare Chocolate Glaze and drizzle over cake. Store leftovers covered in refrigerator.

Fudge Ribbon Cake

Mini Doughnut Cupcakes

1 cup sugar
1½ teaspoons ground cinnamon
1 package (18¼ ounces) yellow or white cake mix, plus ingredients to prepare mix
1 tablespoon ground nutmeg

Makes 24 cupcakes

1. Preheat oven to 350°F. Grease and flour 24 mini (1¾-inch) muffin pan cups. Combine sugar and cinnamon in small bowl; set aside.

2. Prepare cake mix according to package directions; stir nutmeg into batter. Fill prepared muffin cups two-thirds full.

3. Bake about 12 minutes or until lightly browned and toothpick inserted into centers comes out clean.

4. Remove cupcakes from pans; roll in sugar mixture until completely coated. Serve warm or at room temperature.

Pecan Coconut Topped Chocolate Cake

Prep Time: 10 minutes   Cook Time: 40 minutes

1 package (18 ounces) chocolate cake mix
1 cup HELLMANN'S® or BEST FOODS® Real Mayonnaise
1 cup water
3 eggs
1 cup flaked coconut
⅔ cup firmly packed brown sugar
½ cup finely chopped pecans

Makes 12 servings

1. Preheat oven to 350°F. Grease and lightly flour 13×9-inch baking pan; set aside.

2. In large bowl, with electric mixer on low speed, beat cake mix, Hellmann's or Best Foods Real Mayonnaise, water and eggs 30 seconds. Beat on medium speed, scraping sides occasionally, 2 minutes. Pour into prepared pan.

3. In small bowl, combine coconut, brown sugar and pecans. Sprinkle over cake batter.

4. Bake 40 minutes or until toothpick inserted in center comes out clean. On wire rack, cool completely. To serve, cut into squares.

Mini Doughnut Cupcakes

Double Chocolate Chip Snack Cake

1 package (18¼ ounces) devil's food cake mix with pudding in the mix, divided

2 eggs

½ cup water

¼ cup vegetable oil

½ teaspoon cinnamon

1 cup semisweet chocolate chips, divided

¼ cup packed brown sugar

2 tablespoons butter, melted

¾ cup white chocolate chips

Makes 8 to 10 servings

1. Preheat oven to 350°F. Grease 9-inch round cake pan. Reserve ¾ cup cake mix; set aside.

2. Pour remaining cake mix into large bowl. Add eggs, water, oil and cinnamon; beat with electric mixer at medium speed 2 minutes. Remove ½ cup batter; reserve for another use.* Spread remaining batter in prepared pan; sprinkle with ½ cup semisweet chocolate chips.

3. Combine reserved cake mix and brown sugar in medium bowl. Stir in butter and remaining ½ cup semisweet chocolate chips; mix well. Sprinkle mixture over batter in pan.

4. Bake 35 to 40 minutes or until toothpick inserted into center comes out clean and cake springs back when lightly touched. Cool cake in pan on wire rack 10 minutes; remove from pan and cool completely on wire rack.

5. Place white chocolate chips in resealable food storage bag; seal bag. Microwave on HIGH 10 seconds and knead bag gently. Repeat until chips are melted. Cut off ¼ inch from corner of bag with scissors; drizzle chocolate over cake. Let glaze set before cutting cake into wedges.

*If desired, extra batter can be used for cupcakes: Pour batter into two foil or paper baking cups placed on baking sheet; bake at 350°F 20 to 25 minutes or until toothpick inserted into centers comes out clean.

Double Chocolate Chip Snack Cake

Tropical Sunshine Cake

1 package (18.25 ounces) yellow cake mix
1 can (12 fluid ounces) NESTLÉ® CARNATION® Evaporated Milk
2 large eggs
1 can (20 ounces) crushed pineapple in juice, drained (juice reserved), *divided*
½ cup chopped almonds
¾ cup sifted powdered sugar
1 cup flaked coconut, toasted
Whipped cream

Makes 12 servings

PREHEAT oven to 350°F. Grease 13×9-inch baking pan.

COMBINE cake mix, evaporated milk and eggs in large mixer bowl. Beat on low speed for 2 minutes. Stir in *1 cup* pineapple. Pour batter into prepared baking pan. Sprinkle with almonds.

BAKE for 30 to 35 minutes or until wooden pick inserted in center comes out clean. Cool in pan on wire rack for 15 minutes.

COMBINE sugar and 2 tablespoons *reserved* pineapple juice in small bowl; mix until smooth. Spread over warm cake, sprinkle with coconut and *remaining* pineapple. Cool completely before serving. Top with whipped cream.

Upside-Down German Chocolate Cake

1½ cups flaked coconut
1½ cups chopped pecans
1 package DUNCAN HINES® Moist Deluxe® German Chocolate or Classic Chocolate Cake Mix
1 package (8 ounces) cream cheese, softened
½ cup butter or margarine, melted
1 pound (3½ to 4 cups) confectioners' sugar

Makes 12 to 16 servings

1. Preheat oven to 350°F. Grease and flour 13×9-inch baking pan.

2. Spread coconut evenly on bottom of pan. Sprinkle with pecans. Prepare cake mix as directed on package. Pour over coconut and pecans. Combine cream cheese and butter in medium bowl. Beat at low speed with electric mixer until creamy. Add sugar; beat until blended. Drop by spoonfuls evenly over cake batter. Bake at 350°F for 45 to 50 minutes or until toothpick inserted halfway to bottom of cake comes out clean. Cool completely in pan. Cut into individual pieces; turn upside down onto plate.

Tropical Sunshine Cake

Chocolate Chip Cheesecake

1 package DUNCAN HINES® Moist
Deluxe® Devil's Food Cake Mix
½ cup vegetable oil
3 packages (8 ounces each)
cream cheese, softened
1½ cups granulated sugar
1 cup sour cream
1½ teaspoons vanilla extract
4 eggs, lightly beaten
¾ cup mini semisweet chocolate
chips, divided
1 teaspoon all-purpose flour

Makes 12 to 16 servings

1. Preheat oven to 350°F. Grease 10-inch springform pan.

2. Combine cake mix and oil in large bowl. Mix well. Press onto bottom of prepared pan. Bake at 350°F for 22 to 25 minutes or until set. Remove from oven. *Increase oven temperature to 450°F.*

3. Place cream cheese in large mixing bowl. Beat at low speed with electric mixer, adding sugar gradually. Add sour cream and vanilla extract, mixing until blended. Add eggs, mixing only until incorporated. Toss ½ cup chocolate chips with flour. Fold into cream cheese mixture. Pour filling onto crust. Sprinkle with remaining ¼ cup chocolate chips. Bake at 450°F for 5 to 7 minutes. *Reduce oven temperature to 250°F.* Bake at 250°F for 60 to 65 minutes or until set. Loosen cake from side of pan with knife or metal spatula. Cool completely in pan on cooling rack. Refrigerate until ready to serve. Remove side of pan.

Orange Soak Cake

CAKE
1 package DUNCAN HINES®
Moist Deluxe® Orange
Supreme Cake Mix

GLAZE
2 cups confectioners' sugar
⅓ cup orange juice
2 tablespoons butter or margarine,
melted
1 tablespoon water

Makes 12 to 16 servings

1. Preheat oven to 350°F. Grease and flour 13×9×2-inch baking pan.

2. For cake, prepare and bake following package directions for basic recipe. Poke holes in top of warm cake with tines of fork or toothpick.

3. For glaze, combine confectioners' sugar, orange juice, melted butter and water in medium bowl. Pour slowly over top of cake, allowing glaze to soak into warm cake. Cool completely.

Chocolate Chip Cheesecake

Mini Turtle Cupcakes

1 package (21½ ounces) brownie mix plus ingredients to prepare mix
½ cup chopped pecans
1 cup prepared or homemade dark chocolate frosting
½ cup coarsely chopped pecans, toasted*
12 caramels
1 to 2 tablespoons whipping cream

*To toast nuts, spread them on a baking sheet and place in a 350°F oven for 8 to 10 minutes. Or, toast nuts in an ungreased skillet over medium heat until golden brown, stirring frequently. Cool to room temperature before combining with other ingredients.

Makes 54 cupcakes

1. Heat oven to 350°F. Line 54 mini (1½-inch) muffin pan cups with paper baking cups.

2. Prepare brownie batter according to package directions. Stir in chopped pecans.

3. Spoon batter into prepared muffin cups, filling two-thirds full. Bake 18 minutes or until toothpick inserted into centers comes out clean. Cool in pans on wire racks 5 minutes. Remove to wire racks; cool completely.

4. Spread frosting over cooled cupcakes; top with toasted pecans.

5. Combine caramels and 1 tablespoon cream in small saucepan. Cook and stir over low heat until caramels are melted and mixture is smooth. Add additional 1 tablespoon cream if necessary to thin mixture. Spoon caramel decoratively over cupcakes. Store at room temperature up to 24 hours or cover and refrigerate for up to 3 days before serving.

Cinnamon Ripple Cake

1 package DUNCAN HINES® Angel Food Cake Mix
2¼ teaspoons ground cinnamon, divided
1½ cups frozen whipped topping, thawed

Makes 12 to 16 servings

1. Preheat oven to 350°F.

2. Prepare cake following package directions. Spoon one third of batter into ungreased 10-inch tube pan. Spread evenly. Sprinkle 1 teaspoon cinnamon over batter with small fine sieve. Repeat layers. Top with remaining cake batter. Bake and cool following package directions.

3. Mix whipped topping and remaining ¼ teaspoon cinnamon in small bowl. Serve with cake slices.

Mini Turtle Cupcakes

Marbled Angel Cake

1 package (16 ounces) angel food
cake mix
¼ cup HERSHEY'S Cocoa
Chocolate Glaze (recipe follows)

Makes 16 servings

1. Place oven rack in lowest position. Heat oven to 375°F.

2. Prepare cake batter according to package directions. Transfer 4 cups cake batter to medium bowl; gradually fold in cocoa until well blended, being careful not to deflate batter. Alternately pour vanilla and chocolate batters into ungreased 10-inch tube pan. With knife or metal spatula, cut through batters for marble effect.

3. Bake 30 to 35 minutes or until top crust is firm and looks very dry. *Do not underbake.* Invert pan onto heatproof funnel or bottle; cool completely, at least 1½ hours. Carefully run knife along side of pan to loosen cake; remove from pan. Place on serving plate; drizzle with Chocolate Glaze. Let stand until set. Store, covered, at room temperature.

Chocolate Glaze: Combine ⅓ cup sugar and ¼ cup water in small saucepan. Cook over medium heat, stirring constantly, until mixture comes to a boil. Stir until sugar dissolves; remove from heat. Immediately add 1 cup HERSHEY'S MINI CHIPS® Semi-Sweet Chocolate Chips; stir until chips are melted and mixture is smooth. Cool to desired consistency; use immediately.

Marbled Angel Cake

White Chocolate Macadamia Cupcakes

1 package (18¼ ounces) white cake mix, plus ingredients to prepare mix
1 package (4-serving size) white chocolate instant pudding and pie filling mix
¾ cup chopped macadamia nuts
1½ cups flaked coconut
1 cup white chocolate chips
1 container (16 ounces) white frosting

Makes 20 cupcakes

1. Preheat oven to 350°F. Line 20 standard (2½-inch) muffin pan cups with paper baking cups.

2. Prepare cake mix according to package directions, beating in pudding mix with cake mix ingredients. Stir in nuts. Fill muffin cups two-thirds full. Bake 18 to 20 minutes or until toothpick inserted into centers comes out clean. Cool in pans on wire racks 10 minutes. Remove to wire racks; cool completely.

3. Meanwhile, spread coconut evenly on ungreased baking sheet; bake at 350°F 6 minutes, stirring occasionally, until light golden brown. Cool completely.

4. Place white chocolate chips in small microwavable bowl; microwave 2 minutes on MEDIUM (50%), stirring every 30 seconds, until melted and smooth. Cool slightly before stirring into frosting. Frost cupcakes; sprinkle with toasted coconut.

White Chocolate Macadamia Cupcakes

Brownie Sundae Cake

1 (19- to 21-ounce) package fudge
   brownie mix, prepared
   according to package directions
   for cake-like brownies
1 cup "M&M's"® Semi-Sweet
   Chocolate Mini Baking Bits
½ cup chopped nuts, optional
1 quart vanilla ice cream, softened
¼ cup caramel or butterscotch ice
   cream topping

Makes 12 slices

Line 2 (9-inch) round cake pans with aluminum foil, extending slightly over edges of pans. Lightly spray bottoms with vegetable cooking spray; set aside. Preheat oven as brownie mix package directs. Divide brownie batter evenly between pans; sprinkle ½ cup "M&M's"® Semi-Sweet Chocolate Mini Baking Bits and ¼ cup nuts, if desired, over each pan. Bake 23 to 25 minutes or until edges begin to pull away from sides of pan. Cool completely. Remove layers by lifting foil from pans.

To assemble cake, place one brownie layer, topping-side down, in 9-inch springform pan. Carefully spread ice cream over brownie layer; drizzle with ice cream topping. Place second brownie layer on top of ice cream layer, topping-side up; press down lightly. Wrap in plastic wrap; freeze until firm. Remove from freezer about 15 minutes before serving. Remove side of pan. Cut into wedges.

Chocolate Mousse Cake

1 (18.25- or 18.5-ounce) package
   chocolate cake mix
1 (14-ounce) can EAGLE BRAND®
   Sweetened Condensed Milk
   (NOT evaporated milk)
2 (1-ounce) squares unsweetened
   chocolate, melted
½ cup cold water
1 (4-serving size) package instant
   chocolate pudding mix
1 cup (½ pint) whipping cream,
   stiffly whipped

Makes one (9-inch) layer cake

1. Preheat oven to 350°F. Prepare and bake cake mix as package directs for two 9-inch layers. Remove layers from pans; cool.

2. In large bowl, beat EAGLE BRAND® and chocolate until well blended. Gradually beat in water and pudding mix until smooth. Chill 30 minutes. Beat until smooth. Fold in whipped cream. Chill at least one hour.

3. Place one cake layer on serving plate; top with 1½ cups mousse mixture. Top with remaining cake layer. Frost side and top of cake with remaining mousse mixture.

Brownie Sundae Cake

Chocolate Peanut Butter Candy Bars *(page 218)*

deliciously simple
desserts

Butter Pecan Sweet Potato Crunch

2 cans (15 ounces each) PRINCELLA®
     or SUGARY SAM® Cut Sweet
     Potatoes, drained and mashed
1 can (12 ounces) evaporated milk
1 cup sugar
3 eggs
1 tablespoon cinnamon
1 teaspoon vanilla
½ regular-size package yellow
     cake mix (dry)
1 cup chopped pecans
½ cup butter or margarine, melted
     Whipped topping

Makes 15 to 20 servings

Preheat oven to 350°F. In large bowl, combine first six ingredients. Pour sweet potato mixture into greased 13×9-inch baking pan. Sprinkle dry cake mix on top. Cover with chopped pecans. Drizzle melted butter or margarine on top of pecans. Bake about 1 hour or until center is firm. Chill well. Cut into squares. Serve with whipped topping.

Chocolate Peanut Butter Candy Bars

1 package (18¼ ounces) devil's food
     or dark chocolate cake mix
     without pudding in the mix
1 can (5 ounces) evaporated milk
⅓ cup butter, melted
½ cup dry-roasted peanuts
4 packages (1½ ounces each)
     chocolate peanut butter cups,
     coarsely chopped

Makes 2 dozen bars

1. Preheat oven to 350°F. Lightly grease 13×9-inch baking pan.

2. Beat cake mix, evaporated milk and butter in large bowl with electric mixer at medium speed until well blended. (Dough will be stiff.) Spread two thirds of dough in prepared pan. Sprinkle with peanuts.

3. Bake 10 minutes; remove from oven and sprinkle with chopped candy.

4. Drop remaining dough by large spoonfuls over candy. Bake 15 to 20 minutes or until set. Cool completely on wire rack.

Butter Pecan Sweet Potato Crunch

1 (14-ounce) can EAGLE BRAND®
    Sweetened Condensed Milk
    (NOT evaporated milk)
1 to 1¼ cups peanut butter
1 egg
1 teaspoon vanilla extract
2 cups biscuit baking mix
    Granulated sugar

Easy Peanut Butter Cookies

Prep Time: 10 minutes   Bake Time: 6 to 8 minutes

Makes about 5 dozen cookies

1. In large bowl, beat EAGLE BRAND®, peanut butter, egg and vanilla until smooth. Add biscuit mix; mix until well blended. Chill at least 1 hour.

2. Preheat oven to 350°F. Shape dough into 1-inch balls. Roll in sugar. Place 2 inches apart on ungreased baking sheets. Flatten with fork in criss-cross pattern.

3. Bake 6 to 8 minutes or until lightly browned (Do not overbake). Cool. Store tightly covered at room temperature.

Peanut Blossom Cookies: Make dough as directed above. Shape into 1-inch balls and roll in sugar; do not flatten. Bake as directed above. Immediately after baking, press solid milk chocolate candy kiss in center of each cookie.

Peanut Butter & Jelly Gems: Make dough as directed above. Shape into 1-inch balls and roll in sugar; do not flatten. Press thumb in center of each ball of dough; fill with jelly, jam or preserves. Proceed as directed above.

Any-Way-You-Like 'em Cookies: Stir 1 cup semisweet chocolate chips, chopped peanuts, raisins or flaked coconut into dough. Proceed as directed above.

Easy Peanut Butter Cookies

Cranberry Cobbler

2 cans (16 ounces each) sliced
    peaches in light syrup, drained
1 can (16 ounces) whole berry
    cranberry sauce
1 package DUNCAN HINES®
    Cinnamon Swirl Muffin Mix
½ cup chopped pecans
⅓ cup butter or margarine, melted
    Whipped topping or ice cream

Makes 9 servings

1. Preheat oven to 350°F.

2. Cut peach slices in half lengthwise. Combine peach slices and cranberry sauce in *ungreased* 9-inch square pan. Knead swirl packet from Mix for 10 seconds. Squeeze contents evenly over fruit.

3. Combine muffin mix, contents of topping packet from Mix and pecans in large bowl. Add melted butter. Stir until thoroughly blended (mixture will be crumbly). Sprinkle crumbs over fruit. Bake 40 to 45 minutes or until lightly browned and bubbly. Serve warm with whipped topping.

Easy Pumpkin Cream Pie

1 *prepared* 9-inch (6 ounces)
    graham cracker crumb crust
1 can (15 ounces) LIBBY'S® 100%
    Pure Pumpkin
1 package (5.1 ounces) vanilla
    instant pudding and pie
    filling mix
1 cup NESTLÉ® CARNATION®
    Evaporated Milk
1 teaspoon pumpkin pie spice
2 cups (about 6 ounces) frozen
    whipped topping, thawed,
    divided
    Fresh raspberries (optional)

Makes 8 servings

COMBINE pumpkin, pudding mix, milk and pumpkin pie spice in large mixer bowl; beat for 1 minute or until blended. Fold in *1½ cups* whipped topping. Spoon into crust. Freeze for at least 4 hours or until firm. Let stand in refrigerator 1 hour before serving. Garnish with *remaining* whipped topping and raspberries. Serve immediately.

Cranberry Cobbler

Decadent Brownie Pie

Prep Time: 25 minutes   Bake Time: 45 to 50 minutes

1 (9-inch) unbaked pie crust
1 cup (6 ounces) semisweet
  chocolate chips
¼ cup (½ stick) butter or margarine
1 (14-ounce) can EAGLE BRAND®
  Sweetened Condensed Milk
  (NOT evaporated milk)
½ cup biscuit baking mix
2 eggs
1 teaspoon vanilla extract
1 cup chopped nuts
  Vanilla ice cream

Makes 1 (9-inch) pie

1. Preheat oven to 375°F. Bake pie crust 10 minutes; remove from oven. Reduce oven temperature to 325°F.

2. In small saucepan over low heat, melt chocolate chips with butter.

3. In large bowl, beat chocolate mixture, EAGLE BRAND®, biscuit mix, eggs and vanilla until smooth. Add nuts. Pour into baked crust.

4. Bake 35 to 40 minutes or until center is set. Serve warm or at room temperature with ice cream. Store leftovers covered in refrigerator.

Cherry Spice Bars

1 (10-ounce) jar maraschino cherries
1 (18¼-ounce) package spice cake
  mix
¼ cup (½ stick) butter or margarine,
  melted
¼ cup firmly packed brown sugar
¼ cup water
2 eggs

GLAZE
1 cup confectioners' sugar
1 tablespoon lemon juice
1 to 2 teaspoons milk

Makes 2 dozen bars

Drain maraschino cherries; discard juice or save for another use. Cut cherries in half. Combine dry cake mix, melted butter, brown sugar, water and eggs in large mixing bowl; mix with spoon or electric mixer until well blended and smooth. Stir in maraschino cherries. Spread batter into greased 13×9×2-inch baking pan.

Bake in preheated 375°F oven 20 to 25 minutes or until top springs back when lightly touched. Let cool in pan on wire rack.

For glaze, combine confectioners' sugar and lemon juice; stir in enough milk to make thick glaze. Drizzle glaze over bars. Allow glaze to set. Cut into bars. Store up to one week in airtight container with sheets of waxed paper between layers of bars.

Favorite recipe from **Cherry Marketing Institute**

Decadent Brownie Pie

Jam Jam Bars

1 package (18¼ ounces) yellow or white cake mix with pudding in the mix
½ cup (1 stick) butter, melted
1 cup apricot preserves or raspberry jam
1 package (11 ounces) peanut butter and milk chocolate chips

Makes 2 dozen bars

1. Preheat oven to 350°F. Lightly spray 13×9-inch baking pan with nonstick cooking spray.

2. Pour cake mix into large bowl; stir in melted butter until well blended. (Dough will be lumpy.) Remove ½ cup dough to medium bowl. Press remaining dough evenly into prepared pan. Spread preserves in thin layer over dough in pan.

3. Add chips to reserved dough; stir until well mixed. (Dough will remain in small lumps evenly distributed throughout chips.) Sprinkle mixture evenly over preserves.

4. Bake 20 minutes or until lightly browned and bubbling at edges. Cool completely in pan on wire rack.

Rich Chocolate Cream Pie

9-inch baked pastry shell
1 package (6-serving size, about 4.6 ounces) vanilla cook and serve pudding and pie filling mix*
3 cups milk
2 cups (12-ounce package) HERSHEY¦S Semi-Sweet Chocolate Chips
Whipped topping (optional)

*Do not use instant pudding.

Makes about 8 servings

1. Prepare pastry shell as package directs; cool.

2. Prepare pudding mix with milk in saucepan, cooking as directed on package. Remove from heat; immediately add chocolate chips to hot pudding mixture, stirring until chips are melted and mixture is smooth.

3. Pour filling into prepared pastry shell. Place plastic wrap directly onto surface of filling; refrigerate several hours or overnight. Garnish with whipped topping, if desired.

Jam Jam Bars

Strawberries & Cream Dessert

1 (14-ounce) can EAGLE BRAND®
    Sweetened Condensed Milk
    (NOT evaporated milk)
1½ cups cold water
1 (4-serving-size) package vanilla
    instant pudding and pie
    filling mix
2 cups (1 pint) whipping cream,
    whipped
1 (12-ounce) prepared loaf
    pound cake, cut into cubes
    (about 6 cups)
4 cups sliced fresh strawberries
½ cup strawberry preserves
    Additional sliced fresh strawberries
    Toasted slivered almonds

Makes 10 to 12 servings

1. In large bowl, combine EAGLE BRAND® and water; mix well. Add pudding mix; beat until well blended. Chill 5 minutes. Fold in whipped cream.

2. Spoon 2 cups pudding mixture into 4-quart round glass serving bowl; top with half the cake cubes, half the strawberries, half the preserves and half the remaining pudding mixture. Repeat layers of cake cubes, strawberries and preserves; top with remaining pudding mixture. Garnish with additional strawberries and almonds. Chill 4 hours or until set. Store leftovers covered in refrigerator.

Variation: Here is another way to layer this spectacular dessert: Spoon 2 cups pudding mixture into 4-quart round glass serving bowl; top with cake cubes, all of the strawberries, all of the preserves and the remaining pudding mixture. Garnish and chill as directed above.

Fresh Nectarine- Pineapple Cobbler

Prep Time: 20 minutes   Bake Time: 45 minutes

1½ cups fresh DOLE® Tropical Gold®
    Pineapple, cut into chunks
3 cups sliced ripe DOLE® Fresh
    Nectarines or Peaches
½ cup sugar
2 tablespoons all-purpose flour
½ teaspoon ground cinnamon
1 cup buttermilk baking mix
½ cup low-fat milk

Makes 8 servings

• Combine pineapple, nectarines, sugar, flour and cinnamon in 8-inch square glass baking dish; spread fruit evenly in dish.

• Stir together baking mix and milk in small bowl until just combined. Pour over fruit.

• Bake at 400°F 40 to 45 minutes or until fruit is tender and crust is browned.

Strawberries & Cream Dessert

Ice Cream Sandwiches

1 package (18¼ ounces) chocolate
    cake mix with pudding in
    the mix
2 eggs
¼ cup warm water
3 tablespoons butter, melted
1 pint vanilla ice cream, softened
    Colored sugars or sprinkles

Makes 8 sandwiches

1. Preheat oven to 350°F. Lightly spray 13×9-inch pan with nonstick cooking spray. Line pan with foil; spray foil.

2. Beat cake mix, eggs, water and melted butter in large bowl with electric mixer until well blended. (Dough will be thick and sticky.) Spoon dough into prepared pan. Cover with plastic wrap and press dough evenly into pan, using plastic wrap to keep hands from sticking to dough. Remove plastic wrap and prick surface all over with fork (about 40 times) to prevent dough from rising too much.

3. Bake 20 minutes or until toothpick inserted into center comes out clean. Cool in pan on wire rack.

4. Cut cake in half crosswise; remove one half from pan. Spread ice cream evenly over cake half remaining in pan. Top with second half; use foil in pan to wrap up sandwich.

5. Freeze at least 4 hours. Cut into 8 equal pieces; dip cut ends in sugar or sprinkles. Wrap and freeze sandwiches until ready to serve.

Peppermint Ice Cream Sandwiches: Stir ⅓ cup crushed peppermint candies into vanilla ice cream before assembling. Roll ends of sandwiches in additional crushed peppermint candies to coat.

quick tip

Ice cream is often too hard to scoop when it's right out of the freezer. To soften it quickly, place the container of hard-packed ice cream in the microwave and heat at MEDIUM (50% power) for about 20 seconds or just until softened.

Ice Cream Sandwiches

Chocolate Chip-Oat Cookies

1 package (18¼ ounces) yellow
  cake mix
1 teaspoon baking powder
¾ cup vegetable oil
2 eggs
1 teaspoon vanilla
1 cup uncooked old-fashioned oats
¾ cup semisweet chocolate chips

Makes 4 dozen cookies

1. Preheat oven to 350°F. Lightly grease cookie sheets or line with parchment paper.

2. Combine cake mix and baking powder in large bowl. Add oil, eggs and vanilla; beat by hand until well blended. Stir in oats and chocolate chips.

3. Drop dough by slightly rounded tablespoonfuls 2 inches apart onto prepared cookie sheets. Bake 10 minutes or until golden brown. *Do not overbake.*

4. Let cookies stand on cookie sheets 5 minutes; tranfer to wire racks to cool completely.

Maple Walnut Bars

1 package DUNCAN HINES® Moist
  Deluxe® Classic Yellow Cake
  Mix, divided
⅓ cup butter or margarine, melted
4 eggs, divided
1⅓ cups MRS. BUTTERWORTH'S®
  Maple Syrup
⅓ cup packed light brown sugar
½ teaspoon vanilla extract
1 cup chopped walnuts

Makes 24 bars

1. Preheat oven to 350°F. Grease 13×9-inch baking pan.

2. Reserve ⅔ cup cake mix; set aside. Combine remaining cake mix, melted butter and 1 egg in large bowl. Stir until well blended. (Mixture will be crumbly.) Press into prepared pan. Bake 15 to 20 minutes or until light golden brown.

3. Combine reserved cake mix, maple syrup, remaining 3 eggs, sugar and vanilla extract in large mixing bowl. Beat at low speed with electric mixer for 3 minutes. Pour over crust. Sprinkle with walnuts. Bake 30 to 35 minutes or until filling is set. Cool completely in pan. Cut into bars. Store in refrigerator.

Chocolate Chip-Oat Cookies

Lemon Crumb Bars

Prep Time: 30 minutes   Bake Time: 35 minutes

1 (18.25-ounce) package lemon or
    yellow cake mix
½ cup (1 stick) butter or margarine,
    softened
1 egg
2 cups finely crushed saltine crackers
1 (14-ounce) can EAGLE BRAND®
    Sweetened Condensed Milk
    (NOT evaporated milk)
3 egg yolks
½ cup lemon juice from concentrate

Makes 2 to 3 dozen bars

1. Preheat oven to 350°F. In large bowl, combine cake mix, butter and 1 egg with mixer until crumbly. Stir in cracker crumbs. Reserve 2 cups crumb mixture. Press remaining crumb mixture firmly on bottom of greased 13×9-inch baking pan. Bake 15 to 20 minutes or until golden.

2. With mixer or wire whisk beat EAGLE BRAND®, 3 egg yolks and lemon juice. Spread evenly over prepared crust. Top with reserved crumb mixture.

3. Bake 20 minutes longer or until set and top is golden. Cool. Cut into bars. Store leftovers covered in refrigerator.

Peachy Blueberry Crunch

1 package DUNCAN HINES®
    Bakery-Style Blueberry Streusel
    Muffin Mix
4 cups sliced peeled peaches
    (about 4 large)
½ cup water
3 tablespoons packed brown sugar
½ cup chopped pecans
⅓ cup butter or margarine, melted
    Whipped topping or ice cream
    (optional)

Makes 9 servings

1. Preheat oven to 350°F.

2. Rinse blueberries from Mix with cold water and drain.

3. Arrange peach slices in *ungreased* 9-inch square pan. Sprinkle blueberries over peaches. Combine water and sugar in small bowl. Pour over fruit.

4. Combine muffin mix, pecans and melted butter in large bowl. Stir until thoroughly blended (mixture will be crumbly). Sprinkle crumb mixture over fruit. Sprinkle contents of topping packet from Mix over crumb mixture. Bake at 350°F for 50 to 55 minutes or until lightly browned and bubbly. Serve warm with whipped topping, if desired.

Lemon Crumb Bars

Holiday Double Peanut Butter Fudge Cookies

1 can (14 ounces) sweetened condensed milk (not evaporated milk)
¾ cup REESE'S® Creamy Peanut Butter
2 cups all-purpose biscuit baking mix
1 teaspoon vanilla extract
¾ cup REESE'S® Peanut Butter Chips
¼ cup granulated sugar
½ teaspoon red colored sugar
½ teaspoon green colored sugar

Makes about 3½ dozen cookies

1. Heat oven to 375°F.

2. Beat sweetened condensed milk and peanut butter in large bowl with electric mixer on medium speed until smooth. Beat in baking mix and vanilla; stir in peanut butter chips. Set aside.

3. Mix granulated sugar and colored sugars in small bowl. Shape dough into 1-inch balls; roll in sugar. Place 2 inches apart on ungreased cookie sheet; flatten slightly with bottom of glass.

4. Bake 6 to 8 minutes or until very lightly browned (do not overbake). Cool slightly. Remove to wire rack and cool completely. Store in tightly covered container.

Cran-Lemon Coffeecake

1 package (18¼ ounces) yellow cake mix with pudding in the mix
1 cup water
3 eggs
⅓ cup butter, melted and cooled
¼ cup fresh lemon juice
1 tablespoon grated lemon peel
1½ cups coarsely chopped cranberries

Makes 12 servings

1. Preheat oven to 350°F. Grease and flour 12-inch tube pan. Beat cake mix, water, eggs, melted butter, lemon juice and lemon peel in large bowl with electric mixer at low speed 2 minutes. Fold in cranberries. Spread batter evenly in prepared pan.

2. Bake about 55 minutes or until toothpick inserted 1 inch from edge comes out clean. Cool in pan on wire rack 10 minutes. Remove from pan; cool on wire rack. Serve warm or at room temperature.

Holiday Double Peanut Butter Fudge Cookies

Frozen Pudding Cups

Prep Time: 10 minutes   Freeze Time: 3 hours

1 package (4-serving size)
    chocolate instant pudding
    and pie filling mix
5 cups cold low-fat (2%) milk,
    divided
1 package (4-serving size)
    vanilla instant pudding
    and pie filling mix
Fresh sliced strawberries

Makes 8 servings

1. Whisk chocolate pudding mix and 2½ cups milk in medium bowl about 2 minutes. Repeat with vanilla pudding mix and remaining 2½ cups milk in another medium bowl.

2. Divide half of chocolate pudding among 8 plastic cups. Top with half of vanilla pudding. Repeat layers. Cover with plastic wrap; freeze about 3 hours or until firm. Thaw pudding cups at room temperature 1 hour before serving. Top with sliced strawberries.

Dutch Apple Dessert

Prep time: 25 minutes

5 medium apples, peeled, cored
    and sliced
1 (14-ounce) can EAGLE BRAND®
    Sweetened Condensed Milk
    (NOT evaporated milk)
1 teaspoon ground cinnamon
½ cup (1 stick) plus 2 tablespoons
    cold butter or margarine,
    divided
1½ cups biscuit baking mix, divided
½ cup firmly packed brown sugar
½ cup chopped nuts

Makes 6 to 8 servings

1. Preheat oven to 325°F. Grease 9-inch square baking pan. In medium bowl, combine apples, EAGLE BRAND® and cinnamon.

2. In large bowl, cut ½ cup butter into 1 cup biscuit mix until crumbly. Stir in apple mixture. Pour into prepared pan.

3. In small bowl, combine remaining ½ cup biscuit mix and brown sugar. Cut in 2 tablespoons butter until crumbly; add nuts. Sprinkle evenly over apple mixture.

4. Bake 1 hour or until golden. Serve warm with ice cream, if desired. Store leftovers covered in refrigerator.

Microwave Method: In 2-quart round baking dish, prepare as above. Cook on HIGH (100% power) 14 to 15 minutes, rotating dish after 7 minutes. Let stand 5 minutes.

Frozen Pudding Cups

Orange Coffeecake with Streusel Topping

1 package (about 19 ounces)
    cinnamon swirl muffin mix
¾ cup orange juice
1 egg
1 teaspoon grated orange peel
½ cup pecan pieces
½ cup powdered sugar (optional)
1 tablespoon milk (optional)

Makes 9 servings

1. Preheat oven to 400°F. Grease 9-inch square baking pan; set aside.

2. Place muffin mix in large bowl; stir to break up any lumps. Add orange juice, egg and orange peel; stir until just moistened. (Batter will be slightly lumpy.)

3. Knead cinnamon swirl packet 10 seconds. Cut off end of packet; squeeze contents over batter. Swirl into batter using knife or spatula. Do not mix in completely.

4. Spoon batter into prepared pan; sprinkle with topping packet and pecans. Bake 23 to 25 minutes or until toothpick inserted into center comes out almost clean. Cool in pan on wire rack 15 minutes.

5. For icing, combine powdered sugar and milk in small bowl; stir until smooth. Drizzle over cooled coffeecake.

quick tip

For extra flavor and crunch, toast nuts before using them in a recipe. Spread the nuts on a baking sheet and place in a 350°F oven for 8 to 10 minutes. (A small amount of nuts can also be toasted in a toaster oven.) Or, toast nuts in an ungreased skillet over medium heat until golden brown, stirring frequently. Always cool nuts to room temperature before combining them with other ingredients.

Orange Coffeecake with Streusel Topping

Easy Chocolate Coconut Cream Pie

1 (9-inch) pie crust
1 package (4-serving size) vanilla
   cook and serve pudding and
   pie filling mix*
½ cup sugar
¼ cup HERSHEY'S Cocoa or
   HERSHEY'S SPECIAL DARK®
   Cocoa
1¾ cups milk
1 cup MOUNDS® Sweetened
   Coconut Flakes
2 cups frozen whipped topping,
   thawed

Do not use instant pudding mix.

Makes 8 servings

1. Bake pie crust; cool completely.

2. Stir together dry pudding mix, sugar and cocoa in large microwave-safe bowl. Gradually add milk, stirring with whisk until blended.

3. Microwave at HIGH (100%) 6 minutes, stirring with whisk every 2 minutes, until mixture boils and is thickened and smooth. If necessary, microwave an additional 1 minute; stir.

4. Cool 5 minutes in bowl; stir in coconut. Pour into prepared pie crust. Carefully press plastic wrap directly onto pie filling. Cool; refrigerate 6 hours or until firm. Top with whipped topping. Garnish as desired.

Lemon Chiffon

2 packages (4-serving size each)
   lemon gelatin
2 packages (4-serving size each)
   vanilla instant pudding and
   pie filling mix
3 cups boiling water
1 container (8 ounces) frozen
   whipped topping, thawed

Makes 12 servings

1. Combine gelatin and pudding mixes in 5-quart serving bowl. Add boiling water; stir constantly until completely dissolved. Refrigerate about 1 hour or until mixture is chilled and has thickened slightly.

2. Stir in whipped topping; refrigerate at least 1 hour or until set.

Easy Chocolate Coconut Cream Pie

Blueberry Streusel Cobbler

Prep Time: 15 minutes   Bake Time: 1 hour and 10 minutes

1 pint fresh or frozen blueberries
1 (14-ounce) can EAGLE BRAND®
    Sweetened Condensed Milk
    (NOT evaporated milk)
2 teaspoons grated lemon zest
¾ cup (1½ sticks) plus 2 tablespoons
    cold butter or margarine,
    divided
2 cups biscuit baking mix, divided
½ cup firmly packed light brown
    sugar
½ cup chopped nuts
    Vanilla ice cream (optional)
    Blueberry Sauce (recipe follows,
    optional)

Makes 8 to 12 servings

1. Preheat oven to 325°F. In medium bowl, combine blueberries, EAGLE BRAND® and lemon zest.

2. In large bowl, cut ¾ cup butter into 1½ cups biscuit mix until crumbly; stir in blueberry mixture. Spread in greased 9-inch square baking pan.

3. In small bowl, combine remaining ½ cup biscuit mix and brown sugar; cut in remaining 2 tablespoons butter until crumbly. Add nuts. Sprinkle over batter.

4. Bake 65 to 70 minutes. Serve warm with vanilla ice cream and Blueberry Sauce, if desired. Store leftovers covered in refrigerator.

Blueberry Sauce: In medium saucepan over medium heat, combine ½ cup granulated sugar, 1 tablespoon cornstarch, ½ teaspoon ground cinnamon and ¼ teaspoon ground nutmeg. Gradually add ½ cup water; cook and stir until thickened. Stir in 1 pint blueberries; cook and stir until heated through. Makes about 1⅔ cups sauce.

Blueberry Streusel Cobbler

"Mexican" Brownies

1 box (19.8 ounces) brownie mix,
   plus ingredients to prepare mix
2 teaspoons ground cinnamon
1 package (8 ounces) cream cheese,
   softened
½ cup dulce de leche*
2 tablespoons powdered sugar

Dulce de leche is caramelized condensed milk frequently used in Mexican desserts. It is sold in cans in most large supermarkets and in Mexican or Latin grocery stores.

Makes 2 dozen brownies

1. Prepare and bake brownies according to package directions, stirring cinnamon into batter. Cool completely in pan on wire rack.

2. Beat cream cheese in medium bowl with electric mixer at medium speed until smooth. Add dulce de leche and sugar; beat until well blended and creamy.

3. Spread frosting over brownies. Serve immediately or refrigerate overnight for richer flavor.

Mini Custard Fruit Tarts

6 *prepared* single-serving graham
   cracker crumb crusts
1 package (3 ounces) vanilla
   pudding and pie filling mix
   (*not instant*)
⅓ cup water
1 can (12 fluid ounces) NESTLÉ®
   CARNATION® Evaporated
   Lowfat Milk
1 teaspoon grated lemon peel
   Sliced fresh strawberries, kiwi,
   blueberries, raspberries, or
   orange sections (optional)
   Mint leaves (optional)

Makes 6 servings

COMBINE pudding mix and water in small saucepan. Add evaporated milk and lemon peel; stir until smooth. Cook over medium-low heat, stirring constantly, until mixture comes to a boil and thickens.

POUR into crusts; refrigerate for 1 hour or until set. Top with fruit and mint leaves before serving.

Variation: For a Key Lime twist to this recipe, substitute 2 teaspoons fresh lime juice and 1 teaspoon grated lime peel for the grated lemon peel. Top with lime slices.

The publisher would like to thank the companies and organizations listed below for the use of their recipes and photographs in this publication.

ACH Food Companies, Inc.
Allen Canning Company
American Lamb Council
Birds Eye Foods
Bob Evans®
Cabot® Creamery Cooperative
Cherry Marketing Institute
Del Monte Corporation
Dole Food Company, Inc.
Duncan Hines® and Moist Deluxe® are registered trademarks of Pinnacle Foods Corp.
EAGLE BRAND®
The Golden Grain Company®
Heinz North America
The Hershey Company
The Hidden Valley® Food Products Company
Hormel Foods, LLC
Jennie-O Turkey Store®
©Mars, Incorporated 2007
McIlhenny Company (TABASCO® brand Pepper Sauce)
Mrs. Dash®
National Cattlemen's Beef Association on Behalf of The Beef Checkoff
National Pork Board
National Turkey Federation
Nestlé USA
Ortega®, A Division of B&G Foods, Inc.
Perdue Farms Incorporated
Reckitt Benckiser Inc.
Sonoma® Dried Tomatoes
StarKist Seafood Company
Sun•Maid® Growers of California
Unilever

A

Angel Almond Cupcakes, 188
Any-Way-You-Like 'em Cookies, 220
Appetizer Chicken Wings, 14
Apple Pecan Stuffing, 176
Artichokes
   Hidden Valley® Torta, 26
   Melted Brie & Artichoke Dip, 20
Asian Noodles with Vegetables and Chicken, 86
Asian Shrimp & Noodle Salad, 68
Asparagus
   Bistro Chicken Skillet, 90
   Chicken, Asparagus & Mushroom Bake, 102
   Scallop Stir-Fry, 90
Avocado Ranch Soup, 52

B

Baja Fish Tacos, 150
Baked Penne & Ham, 94
Baked Spinach Feta Dip, 8
Bayou Dirty Rice, 170
Bayou-Style Pot Pie, 116
Beans
   Black and White Chili, 156
   Crunchy Layered Beef & Bean Salad, 58
   Easy Cajun Chicken Stew, 36
   Fast 'n Easy Chili, 88
   First Alarm Chili, 88
   Hearty Meatless Chili, 144
   Hearty Nachos, 20
   Jamaican Pork Skillet, 104
   Louisiana Red Beans & Rice, 178
   Mexicali Vegetable Soup, 54
   Pork Chop & Wild Rice Bake, 88
   Refried Bean Tostadas, 140

Beans *(continued)*
   Second Alarm Chili, 88
   Southwestern Chicken Taco Salad, 74
   Southwestern Rice, 162
   Spicy Chicken Casserole with Cornbread, 108
   Super Chili for a Crowd, 122
   Texas Ranch Chili Beans, 172
   Tex-Mex Chicken & Rice Chili, 134
   Third Alarm Chili, 88
   Vegetable Hummus, 16
   Vegetarian Chili with Cornbread Topping, 114
   White Chicken Chili, 148
Beef *(see also* **Beef, Ground**)
   Beef in Wine Sauce, 84
   Classic Fajitas, 154
   Greek Isle Rice Salad, 60
   Harvest Pot Roast with Sweet Potatoes, 132
   Hearty BBQ Beef Sandwiches, 138
   Mushroom-Beef Stew, 32
   Oriental Steak Salad, 80
   Oven-Baked Stew, 54
   Skillet Beef & Broccoli, 110
   Southwestern Beef Stew, 40
   Super Chili for a Crowd, 122
   Tex-Mex Flank Steak Salad, 64
   Thai-Style Beef & Rice, 100
   Zesty Steak Fajitas, 124
Beef in Wine Sauce, 84
Beef, Ground
   Bite-Size Tacos, 6
   Crunchy Layered Beef & Bean Salad, 58
   Empanada Pie, 94
   Fast 'n Easy Chili, 88
   First Alarm Chili, 88
   Grilled Reuben Burger, 128

Beef, Ground *(continued)*
   Hearty Nachos, 20
   Mexicali Vegetable Soup, 54
   Mini Taco Quiches, 16
   Pizza Meat Loaf, 148
   Quick Taco Macaroni & Cheese, 84
   Second Alarm Chili, 88
   Spinach & Feta Burgers, 138
   Super Chili for a Crowd, 122
   Third Alarm Chili, 88
Beer Cheese Dip, 12
Berries
   Biscuit and Sausage Bake, 92
   Blueberry Sauce, 244
   Blueberry Streusel Cobbler, 244
   Cran-Lemon Coffeecake, 236
   Flower Power Strawberry Cake, 194
   Peachy Blueberry Crunch, 234
   Raspberry Buckle Cupcakes, 196
   Strawberries & Cream Dessert, 228
Biscuit and Sausage Bake, 92
Bistro Chicken Skillet, 90
Bite-Size Tacos, 6
Black and White Chili, 156
Blueberry Sauce, 244
Blueberry Streusel Cobbler, 244
Bouillabaisse, 34
Breads
   Oniony Corn Spoonbread, 184
   Pizza Biscuits, 180
   Savory Rosemary Quick Bread, 182
   Southwestern Sausage Drop Biscuits, 168
   Spinach Spoonbread, 174

Breads (continued)
Super-Moist Cornbread, 172
Tomato Cheese Bread, 164
Broccoli
Broccoli-Stuffed Shells, 104
Broccoli, Turkey and Noodle
Skillet, 100
Cheddar Broccoli Quiche,
142
Easy Asian Chicken Skillet,
110
Savory Skillet Broccoli, 178
Skillet Beef & Broccoli, 110
Broccoli-Stuffed Shells, 104
Broccoli, Turkey and Noodle
Skillet, 100
Brownie Sundae Cake, 214
Butter Pecan Sweet Potato
Crunch, 218

C
Cakes
Brownie Sundae Cake, 214
Butter Pecan Sweet Potato
Crunch, 218
Chocolate Chip Cheesecake,
206
Chocolate Mousse Cake,
214
Cinnamon Ripple Cake, 208
Cran-Lemon Coffeecake, 236
Double Chocolate Chip
Snack Cake, 202
Flower Power Strawberry
Cake, 194
Fudge Ribbon Bundt Cake,
198
Fudge Ribbon Cake, 198
Marbled Angel Cake, 210
Orange Coffeecake with
Streusel Topping, 240
Orange Glow Bundt Cake,
190
Orange Soak Cake, 206

Cakes (continued)
Peach Cream Cake, 188
Pecan Coconut Topped
Chocolate Cake, 200
Pumpkin Crunch Cake, 196
Tropical Sunshine Cake,
204
Upside-Down German
Chocolate Cake, 204
California Crab Salad, 58
Cheddar Broccoli Quiche, 142
Cheddary Mashed Potato Bake,
160
Cheese Ravioli Soup, 46
Cheesy Baked Potatoes, 164
Cherries
Cherry Spice Bars, 224
Chicken, Cherry and Wild Rice
Salad, 66
Spiced Turkey with Fruit Salsa,
122
Cherry Spice Bars, 224
Chicken (see also **Chicken,
Boneless; Chicken,
Cooked**)
Appetizer Chicken Wings,
14
Bistro Chicken Skillet, 90
Coq au Vin & Pasta, 98
Country Chicken Stew with
Dumplings, 44
Country Roasted Chicken
Dinner, 152
Crispy Tortilla Chicken, 12
Mustard-Crusted Chicken &
Rice, 126
Ranch Drummettes, 22
Saffron Chicken & Vegetables,
112
The Original Ranch® Crispy
Chicken, 140
White Chicken Chili, 148
Chicken and Wild Rice Soup,
48

Chicken, Asparagus & Mushroom
Bake, 102
Chicken, Boneless
Bayou-Style Pot Pie, 116
Black and White Chili, 156
Chicken and Wild Rice Soup,
48
Chicken, Asparagus &
Mushroom Bake, 102
Chicken Gumbo, 52
Easy Asian Chicken Skillet, 110
Indian-Spiced Chicken with
Wild Rice, 118
Savory Chicken Satay, 8
Spicy Chicken Casserole with
Cornbread, 108
Thai Noodle Soup, 42
Chicken, Cherry and Wild Rice
Salad, 66
Chicken, Cooked
Asian Noodles with Vegetables
and Chicken, 86
Chicken, Cherry and Wild Rice
Salad, 66
Chicken Florentine in Minutes,
96
Easy Cajun Chicken Stew, 36
Hidden Valley® Chopstick
Chicken Salad, 66
Pineapple Chicken Salad, 60
Primavera Light, 114
Quick Chicken Stew with
Biscuits, 38
Quick Hot and Sour Chicken
Soup, 32
Refreshing Chicken & Rice
Salad, 78
Santa Fe Rice Salad, 70
Sonoma® Pot Pie, 136
Southwestern Chicken Taco
Salad, 74
Tex-Mex Chicken & Rice Chili,
134
30-Minute Paella, 106

Chicken Florentine in Minutes, 96
Chicken Gumbo, 52
Chili
Black and White Chili, 156
Fast 'n Easy Chili, 88
First Alarm Chili, 88
Hearty Meatless Chili, 144
Mexican Turkey Chili Mac, 106
Second Alarm Chili, 88
Super Chili for a Crowd, 122
Texas Ranch Chili Beans, 172
Tex-Mex Chicken & Rice Chili, 134
Third Alarm Chili, 88
Vegetarian Chili with Cornbread Topping, 114
White Chicken Chili, 148
Chocolate
Any-Way-You-Like 'em Cookies, 220
Brownie Sundae Cake, 214
Chocolate Chip Cheesecake, 206
Chocolate Chip-Oat Cookies, 232
Chocolate Glaze, 198, 210
Chocolate Mousse Cake, 214
Chocolate Peanut Butter Candy Bars, 218
Chocolate Tiramisu Cupcakes, 192
Decadent Brownie Pie, 224
Double Chocolate Chip Snack Cake, 202
Easy Chocolate Coconut Cream Pie, 242
Frozen Pudding Cups, 238
Fudge Ribbon Bundt Cake, 198

Chocolate (continued)
Fudge Ribbon Cake, 198
Holiday Double Peanut Butter Fudge Cookies, 236
Ice Cream Sandwiches, 230
Jam Jam Bars, 226
Marbled Angel Cake, 210
"Mexican" Brownies, 246
Mini Turtle Cupcakes, 208
Peanut Blossom Cookies, 220
Pecan Coconut Topped Chocolate Cake, 200
Peppermint Ice Cream Sandwiches, 230
Rich Chocolate Cream Pie, 226
Upside-Down German Chocolate Cake, 204
White Chocolate Macadamia Cupcakes, 212
Chocolate Chip Cheesecake, 206
Chocolate Chip-Oat Cookies, 232
Chocolate Glaze, 198, 210
Chocolate Mousse Cake, 214
Chocolate Peanut Butter Candy Bars, 218
Chocolate Tiramisu Cupcakes, 192
Cinnamon Ripple Cake, 208
Classic Fajitas, 154
Coconut
Easy Chocolate Coconut Cream Pie, 242
Pecan Coconut Topped Chocolate Cake, 200
Tropical Sunshine Cake, 204
Upside-Down German Chocolate Cake, 204
White Chocolate Macadamia Cupcakes, 212
Confetti Wild Rice Salad, 72

Cookies & Bars
Any-Way-You-Like 'em Cookies, 220
Cherry Spice Bars, 224
Chocolate Chip-Oat Cookies, 232
Chocolate Peanut Butter Candy Bars, 218
Easy Peanut Butter Cookies, 220
Holiday Double Peanut Butter Fudge Cookies, 236
Jam Jam Bars, 226
Lemon Crumb Bars, 234
Maple Walnut Bars, 232
"Mexican" Brownies, 246
Peanut Blossom Cookies, 220
Peanut Butter & Jelly Gems, 220
Coq au Vin & Pasta, 98
Corn
Hearty Corn & Cheese Chowder, 34
Home-Style Corn Cakes, 24
Jamaican Pork Skillet, 104
Mexican Turkey Chili Mac, 106
Oniony Corn Spoonbread, 184
Santa Fe Rice Salad, 70
Southern Pecan Cornbread Stuffing, 160
Southwestern Beef Stew, 40
Southwestern Chicken Taco Salad, 74
Southwestern Rice, 162
Southwestern Turkey Stew, 50
Spicy Chicken Casserole with Cornbread, 108
Super-Moist Cornbread, 172
Country Chicken Stew with Dumplings, 44
Country Pork Skillet, 86

Country Roasted Chicken Dinner, 152
Cranberry Cobbler, 222
Cranberry-Onion Pork Roast, 136
Cran-Lemon Coffeecake, 236
Creamed Spinach, 170
Creamy Leek Chowder, 42
Creole Shrimp and Rice, 98
Crispy Tortilla Chicken, 12
Crunchy Layered Beef & Bean Salad, 58

Cupcakes
Angel Almond Cupcakes, 188
Chocolate Tiramisu Cupcakes, 192
Mini Doughnut Cupcakes, 200
Mini Turtle Cupcakes, 208
Raspberry Buckle Cupcakes, 196
White Chocolate Macadamia Cupcakes, 212

Curried Shrimp and Noodles, 126

D
Decadent Brownie Pie, 224
Dips & Spreads
Baked Spinach Feta Dip, 8
Beer Cheese Dip, 12
Hidden Valley® Salsa Ranch Dip, 18
Hidden Valley® Torta, 26
Melted Brie & Artichoke Dip, 20
Original Ranch® Spinach Dip, 10
Pecan Cheese Ball, 28
Roasted Red Pepper Spread, 6
7-Layer Ranch Dip, 28
Vegetable Hummus, 16

Double Chocolate Chip Snack Cake, 202
Dutch Apple Dessert, 238

E
Easy Asian Chicken Skillet, 110
Easy Cajun Chicken Stew, 36
Easy Cheese & Tomato Macaroni, 130
Easy Chocolate Coconut Cream Pie, 242
Easy Fried Rice, 174
Easy Peanut Butter Cookies, 220
Easy Pumpkin Cream Pie, 222
Empanada Pie, 94

F
Fast 'n Easy Chili, 88
Fiesta Party Mix, 26
First Alarm Chili, 88
Fish
Baja Fish Tacos, 150
Bouillabaisse, 34
Hidden Valley® Broiled Fish, 146
Tuna and Rice Skillet Dinner, 116
Tuna Ramen Noodle Salad, 76

Flower Power Strawberry Cake, 194
Fresh Nectarine-Pineapple Cobbler, 228
Frozen Pudding Cups, 238
Fudge Ribbon Bundt Cake, 198
Fudge Ribbon Cake, 198

G
Garlic Mashed Potatoes, 182
Garlic Shrimp with Wilted Spinach, 92
Greek Isle Rice Salad, 60

Grilled Mesquite Vegetables, 162
Grilled Potato Salad, 64
Grilled Reuben Burger, 128

H
Ham
Baked Penne & Ham, 94
Pizza Biscuits, 180
Harvest Pot Roast with Sweet Potatoes, 132
Hash Brown Bake, 184
Hearty BBQ Beef Sandwiches, 138
Hearty Corn & Cheese Chowder, 34
Hearty Meatless Chili, 144
Hearty Nachos, 20
Heinz® "TK" Tacoz, 132
Hidden Valley® Broiled Fish, 146
Hidden Valley® Chopstick Chicken Salad, 66
Hidden Valley® Glazed Baby Carrots, 176
Hidden Valley® Salsa Ranch Dip, 18
Hidden Valley® Torta, 26
Holiday Double Peanut Butter Fudge Cookies, 236
Holiday Wild Rice Pilaf, 180
Home-Style Corn Cakes, 24
Homestyle Spinach and Mushrooms, 166

I
Ice Cream Sandwiches, 230
Indian-Spiced Chicken with Wild Rice, 118
Italian Vegetable Soup, 36

J
Jam Jam Bars, 226
Jamaican Pork Skillet, 104

L

Lemon
Cran-Lemon Coffeecake, 236
Lemon Chiffon, 242
Lemon Crumb Bars, 234
Lemon Chiffon, 242
Lemon Crumb Bars, 234
Louisiana Red Beans & Rice, 178

M

Maple Walnut Bars, 232
Marbled Angel Cake, 210
Meatball & Pasta Soup, 48
Mediterranean Orzo Salad, 72
Melted Brie & Artichoke Dip, 20
Mexicali Vegetable Soup, 54
"Mexican" Brownies, 246
Mexican Turkey Chili Mac, 106
Mini Custard Fruit Tarts, 246
Mini Doughnut Cupcakes, 200
Mini Taco Quiches, 16
Mini Turtle Cupcakes, 208
Mushroom-Beef Stew, 32
Mushrooms
Asian Noodles with Vegetables and Chicken, 86
Beef in Wine Sauce, 84
Chicken, Asparagus & Mushroom Bake, 102
Coq au Vin & Pasta, 98
Homestyle Spinach and Mushrooms, 166
Mushroom-Beef Stew, 32
Oven-Baked Stew, 54
Ranch Clam Chowder, 38
Sonoma® Pot Pie, 136
Mustard-Crusted Chicken & Rice, 126

N

Nuts (*see also* **Pecans**)
Blueberry Streusel Cobbler, 244
Chocolate Peanut Butter Candy Bars, 218
Decadent Brownie Pie, 224
Dutch Apple Dessert, 238
Fiesta Party Mix, 26
Maple Walnut Bars, 232
Orange Coffeecake with Streusel Topping, 240
Tropical Sunshine Cake, 204
White Chocolate Macadamia Cupcakes, 212

O

Okra
Creole Shrimp and Rice, 98
Southwestern Beef Stew, 40
Onion-Apple Glazed Pork Tenderloin, 156
Onion-Baked Pork Chops, 150
Onion-Roasted Potatoes, 168
Oniony Corn Spoonbread, 184
Orange
Orange Coffeecake with Streusel Topping, 240
Orange Glow Bundt Cake, 190
Orange Soak Cake, 206
Tex-Mex Flank Steak Salad, 64
Orange Coffeecake with Streusel Topping, 240
Orange Glow Bundt Cake, 190
Orange Soak Cake, 206
Oriental Steak Salad, 80
Original Ranch® Spinach Dip, 10
Original Ranch® Winter Vegetable Salad, 78
Oven-Baked Stew, 54

P

Panzanella, 62
Parsley Dumplings, 44
Party Stuffed Pinwheels, 14
Pasta
Asian Noodles with Vegetables and Chicken, 86
Asian Shrimp & Noodle Salad, 68
Baked Penne & Ham, 94
Bistro Chicken Skillet, 90
Broccoli-Stuffed Shells, 104
Broccoli, Turkey and Noodle Skillet, 100
Cheese Ravioli Soup, 46
Chicken Florentine in Minutes, 96
Coq au Vin & Pasta, 98
Curried Shrimp and Noodles, 126
Easy Asian Chicken Skillet, 110
Easy Cheese & Tomato Macaroni, 130
Hearty Corn & Cheese Chowder, 34
Meatball & Pasta Soup, 48
Mediterranean Orzo Salad, 72
Mexican Turkey Chili Mac, 106
Oriental Steak Salad, 80
Oven-Baked Stew, 54
Panzanella, 62
Pesto Turkey & Pasta, 142
Primavera Light, 114
Quick Taco Macaroni & Cheese, 84
Saucepot Spinach Lasagne, 124
Scallop Stir-Fry, 90
Shrimp Alfredo with Sugar Snap Peas, 130

Pasta (continued)
Shrimp and Pepper Noodle
Bowl, 144
Thai Noodle Soup, 42
Thai Noodles with Peanut
Sauce, 128
Tuna Ramen Noodle Salad,
76
Turkey Fettuccini, 146
Patrick's Irish Lamb Soup, 46
Peach Cream Cake, 188
Peaches
Cranberry Cobbler, 222
Peach Cream Cake, 188
Peachy Blueberry Crunch,
234
Peachy Blueberry Crunch, 234
Peanut Blossom Cookies, 220
Peanut Butter
Any-Way-You-Like 'em Cookies,
220
Chocolate Peanut Butter Candy
Bars, 218
Easy Peanut Butter Cookies,
220
Holiday Double Peanut Butter
Fudge Cookies, 236
Jam Jam Bars, 226
Peanut Blossom Cookies,
220
Peanut Butter & Jelly Gems,
220
Thai Noodles with Peanut
Sauce, 128
Peanut Butter & Jelly Gems,
220
Pecan Cheese Ball, 28
Pecan Coconut Topped Chocolate
Cake, 200
Pecans
Apple Pecan Stuffing, 176
Butter Pecan Sweet Potato
Crunch, 218
Cranberry Cobbler, 222

Pecans (continued)
Mini Turtle Cupcakes, 208
Peachy Blueberry Crunch,
234
Pecan Cheese Ball, 28
Pecan Coconut Topped
Chocolate Cake, 200
Southern Pecan Cornbread
Stuffing, 160
Upside-Down German
Chocolate Cake, 204
Peppered Pork & Pilaf, 96
Peppermint Ice Cream
Sandwiches, 230
Pesto Turkey & Pasta, 142
Pies
Bayou-Style Pot Pie, 116
Decadent Brownie Pie, 224
Easy Chocolate Coconut
Cream Pie, 242
Easy Pumpkin Cream Pie,
222
Empanada Pie, 94
Rich Chocolate Cream Pie,
226
Sonoma® Pot Pie, 136
Pineapple
Fresh Nectarine-Pineapple
Cobbler, 228
Pineapple Chicken Salad,
60
Tropical Sunshine Cake, 204
Pineapple Chicken Salad, 60
Pizza Biscuits, 180
Pizza Meat Loaf, 148
Pork
Country Pork Skillet, 86
Cranberry-Onion Pork Roast,
136
Jamaican Pork Skillet, 104
Onion-Apple Glazed Pork
Tenderloin, 156
Onion-Baked Pork Chops,
150

Pork (continued)
Peppered Pork & Pilaf, 96
Pork Chop & Wild Rice Bake,
88
Pork Chop & Wild Rice Bake,
88
Potato Skins, 22
Potatoes
Butter Pecan Sweet Potato
Crunch, 218
Cheddary Mashed Potato
Bake, 160
Cheesy Baked Potatoes, 164
Country Pork Skillet, 86
Country Roasted Chicken
Dinner, 152
Creamy Leek Chowder, 42
Garlic Mashed Potatoes, 182
Grilled Potato Salad, 64
Harvest Pot Roast with Sweet
Potatoes, 132
Hash Brown Bake, 184
Onion-Roasted Potatoes, 168
Patrick's Irish Lamb Soup, 46
Potato Skins, 22
Vegetable Potato Salad, 70
Primavera Light, 114
Pumpkin
Easy Pumpkin Cream Pie,
222
Pumpkin Crunch Cake, 196
Pumpkin Crunch Cake, 196

Q
Quick Chicken Stew with Biscuits,
38
Quick Hot and Sour Chicken
Soup, 32
Quick Taco Macaroni & Cheese,
84

R
Ranch Clam Chowder, 38
Ranch Drummettes, 22

Raspberry Buckle Cupcakes, 196
Refreshing Chicken & Rice Salad, 78
Refried Bean Tostadas, 140
Rice
Bayou Dirty Rice, 170
California Crab Salad, 58
Chicken and Wild Rice Soup, 48
Chicken, Cherry and Wild Rice Salad, 66
Chicken Gumbo, 52
Confetti Wild Rice Salad, 72
Creole Shrimp and Rice, 98
Easy Cajun Chicken Stew, 36
Easy Fried Rice, 174
Greek Isle Rice Salad, 60
Holiday Wild Rice Pilaf, 180
Indian-Spiced Chicken with Wild Rice, 118
Louisiana Red Beans & Rice, 178
Mustard-Crusted Chicken & Rice, 126
Peppered Pork & Pilaf, 96
Pork Chop & Wild Rice Bake, 88
Quick Hot and Sour Chicken Soup, 32
Refreshing Chicken & Rice Salad, 78
Saffron Chicken & Vegetables, 112
Santa Fe Rice Salad, 70
Southwestern Rice, 162
Southwestern Turkey Stew, 50
Tex-Mex Chicken & Rice Chili, 134
Thai-Style Beef & Rice, 100

Rice (continued)
Tuna and Rice Skillet Dinner, 116
Wild Rice and Vegetable Salad, 62
Rich Chocolate Cream Pie, 226
Roasted Red Pepper Spread, 6

S
Saffron Chicken & Vegetables, 112
Salads (see pages 56–81)
Sandwiches
Grilled Reuben Burger, 128
Hearty BBQ Beef Sandwiches, 138
Ice Cream Sandwiches, 230
Peppermint Ice Cream Sandwiches, 230
Spinach & Feta Burgers, 138
Santa Fe Rice Salad, 70
Saucepot Spinach Lasagne, 124
Sausage
Bayou Dirty Rice, 170
Bayou-Style Pot Pie, 116
Biscuit and Sausage Bake, 92
Panzanella, 62
Sausage Cheese Puffs, 18
Sausage Pinwheels, 10
Southwestern Sausage Drop Biscuits, 168
Sausage Cheese Puffs, 18
Sausage Pinwheels, 10
Savory Chicken Satay, 8
Savory Rosemary Quick Bread, 182
Savory Skillet Broccoli, 178
Scallop Stir-Fry, 90
Second Alarm Chili, 88
7-Layer Ranch Dip, 28
Shellfish (see also **Shrimp**)
Bouillabaisse, 34
California Crab Salad, 58

Shellfish (continued)
Ranch Clam Chowder, 38
Scallop Stir-Fry, 90
Shrimp
Asian Shrimp & Noodle Salad, 68
Creole Shrimp and Rice, 98
Curried Shrimp and Noodles, 126
Garlic Shrimp with Wilted Spinach, 92
Shrimp Alfredo with Sugar Snap Peas, 130
Shrimp and Pepper Noodle Bowl, 144
30-Minute Paella, 106
Shrimp Alfredo with Sugar Snap Peas, 130
Shrimp and Pepper Noodle Bowl, 144
Skillet Beef & Broccoli, 110
Sonoma® Pot Pie, 136
Soups
Avocado Ranch Soup, 52
Bouillabaisse, 34
Cheese Ravioli Soup, 46
Chicken and Wild Rice Soup, 48
Creamy Leek Chowder, 42
Hearty Corn & Cheese Chowder, 34
Italian Vegetable Soup, 36
Meatball & Pasta Soup, 48
Mexicali Vegetable Soup, 54
Patrick's Irish Lamb Soup, 46
Quick Hot and Sour Chicken Soup, 32
Ranch Clam Chowder, 38
Thai Noodle Soup, 42
Southern Pecan Cornbread Stuffing, 160
Southwestern Beef Stew, 40
Southwestern Chicken Taco Salad, 74

Southwestern Rice, 162
Southwestern Sausage Drop
    Biscuits, 168
Southwestern Turkey Stew, 50
Spiced Turkey with Fruit Salsa,
    122
Spicy Chicken Casserole with
    Cornbread, 108
Spinach
    Baked Spinach Feta Dip, 8
    Chicken Florentine in Minutes,
        96
    Creamed Spinach, 170
    Garlic Shrimp with Wilted
        Spinach, 92
    Homestyle Spinach and
        Mushrooms, 166
    Meatball & Pasta Soup, 48
    Original Ranch® Spinach Dip,
        10
    Saucepot Spinach Lasagne,
        124
    Spinach & Feta Burgers,
        138
    Spinach Spoonbread, 174
Spinach & Feta Burgers, 138
Spinach Spoonbread, 174
Squash
    Grilled Mesquite Vegetables,
        162
    Italian Vegetable Soup, 36
    Mexicali Vegetable Soup,
        54
    Stovetop Summer Squash,
        166
    Vegetarian Chili with
        Cornbread Topping, 114
Stews
    Chicken Gumbo, 52
    Country Chicken Stew with
        Dumplings, 44
    Easy Cajun Chicken Stew, 36
    Mushroom-Beef Stew, 32
    Oven-Baked Stew, 54

Stews *(continued)*
    Quick Chicken Stew with
        Biscuits, 38
    Southwestern Beef Stew, 40
    Southwestern Turkey Stew,
        50
    Stovetop Summer Squash, 166
    Strawberries & Cream Dessert,
        228
Stuffing
    Apple Pecan Stuffing, 176
    Chicken, Asparagus &
        Mushroom Bake, 102
    Southern Pecan Cornbread
        Stuffing, 160
    Stovetop Summer Squash,
        166
Super Chili for a Crowd, 122
Super-Moist Cornbread, 172
Sweet & Tangy Marinated
    Vegetables, 76

T
Texas Ranch Chili Beans, 172
Tex-Mex Chicken & Rice Chili,
    134
Tex-Mex Flank Steak Salad, 64
Thai Noodle Soup, 42
Thai Noodles with Peanut Sauce,
    128
Thai-Style Beef & Rice, 100
The Original Ranch® Crispy
    Chicken, 140
Third Alarm Chili, 88
30-Minute Paella, 106
Tomato Cheese Bread, 164
Tropical Sunshine Cake, 204
Tuna and Rice Skillet Dinner,
    116
Tuna Ramen Noodle Salad, 76
Turkey
    Broccoli, Turkey and Noodle
        Skillet, 100
    Heinz® "TK" Tacoz, 132

Turkey *(continued)*
    Mexican Turkey Chili Mac,
        106
    Pesto Turkey & Pasta, 142
    Southwestern Turkey Stew,
        50
    Spiced Turkey with Fruit Salsa,
        122
    Turkey Fettuccini, 146
Turkey Fettuccini, 146

U
Upside-Down German Chocolate
    Cake, 204

V
Vegetable Hummus, 16
Vegetable Potato Salad, 70
Vegetarian Chili with Cornbread
    Topping, 114

W
White Chicken Chili, 148
White Chocolate Macadamia
    Cupcakes, 212
Wild Rice and Vegetable Salad,
    62

Z
Zesty Steak Fajitas, 124

METRIC CONVERSION CHART

VOLUME MEASUREMENTS (dry)

$\frac{1}{8}$ teaspoon = 0.5 mL
$\frac{1}{4}$ teaspoon = 1 mL
$\frac{1}{2}$ teaspoon = 2 mL
$\frac{3}{4}$ teaspoon = 4 mL
1 teaspoon = 5 mL
1 tablespoon = 15 mL
2 tablespoons = 30 mL
$\frac{1}{4}$ cup = 60 mL
$\frac{1}{3}$ cup = 75 mL
$\frac{1}{2}$ cup = 125 mL
$\frac{2}{3}$ cup = 150 mL
$\frac{3}{4}$ cup = 175 mL
1 cup = 250 mL
2 cups = 1 pint = 500 mL
3 cups = 750 mL
4 cups = 1 quart = 1 L

VOLUME MEASUREMENTS (fluid)

1 fluid ounce (2 tablespoons) = 30 mL
4 fluid ounces ($\frac{1}{2}$ cup) = 125 mL
8 fluid ounces (1 cup) = 250 mL
12 fluid ounces (1$\frac{1}{2}$ cups) = 375 mL
16 fluid ounces (2 cups) = 500 mL

WEIGHTS (mass)

$\frac{1}{2}$ ounce = 15 g
1 ounce = 30 g
3 ounces = 90 g
4 ounces = 120 g
8 ounces = 225 g
10 ounces = 285 g
12 ounces = 360 g
16 ounces = 1 pound = 450 g

DIMENSIONS

$\frac{1}{16}$ inch = 2 mm
$\frac{1}{8}$ inch = 3 mm
$\frac{1}{4}$ inch = 6 mm
$\frac{1}{2}$ inch = 1.5 cm
$\frac{3}{4}$ inch = 2 cm
1 inch = 2.5 cm

OVEN TEMPERATURES

250°F = 120°C
275°F = 140°C
300°F = 150°C
325°F = 160°C
350°F = 180°C
375°F = 190°C
400°F = 200°C
425°F = 220°C
450°F = 230°C

BAKING PAN SIZES

Utensil	Size in Inches/Quarts	Metric Volume	Size in Centimeters
Baking or Cake Pan (square or rectangular)	8×8×2	2 L	20×20×5
	9×9×2	2.5 L	23×23×5
	12×8×2	3 L	30×20×5
	13×9×2	3.5 L	33×23×5
Loaf Pan	8×4×3	1.5 L	20×10×7
	9×5×3	2 L	23×13×7
Round Layer Cake Pan	8×1½	1.2 L	20×4
	9×1½	1.5 L	23×4
Pie Plate	8×1¼	750 mL	20×3
	9×1¼	1 L	23×3
Baking Dish or Casserole	1 quart	1 L	—
	1½ quart	1.5 L	—
	2 quart	2 L	—